Alone!

McDougal & Associates

Servants of Christ and stewards of the mysteries of God

NEVER ALONE!

Lessons Learned from a
Consecrated Woman

---

by

Daniel Roberts

All Scripture quotations are from the
Authorized King James Version of the Bible.

NEVER ALONE!
Copyright © 2008—by Daniel Roberts
ALL RIGHTS RESERVED

Original cover design by Sherie Campbell
sonandshield@comcast.net

Published by:

McDougal & Associates
www.thepublishedword.com

McDougal & Associates is dedicated to the spreading of the Gospel of
Jesus Christ to as many people as possible in the shortest time possible.

ISBN 13: 978-1-934769-13-3
ISBN 10: 1-934769-13-4

Printed in the United States of America
For Worldwide Distribution

DEDICATION

To the memory of Wendy Roberts (1950-2007):

I met her in 1976 while ministering at the Goldwater Memorial Hospital in New York City. She had lost her mother to cancer the year before, and that experience, I believe, had made her heart tender toward the Gospel. That next spring she found Christ in a home prayer and Bible study meeting. Her best friend, Jocelyn Mattox (now pastoring in Florida), invited her. Wendy went to the meeting only because Jocelyn was a good cook and told her there would be some good food served at the end of the meeting.

The Bible teacher that night was Evangelist Jackie McCullah (now pastoring a church in upstate New York). I don't know exactly what Jackie said that night, but at the close of the meeting, Wendy accepted Christ, and Jocelyn and Jackie became her first mentors in discipleship. Wendy and I met just a few months later, and I was privileged to be there the day she was baptized in water.

Something drew me to this woman, despite the differences in our background. I was born, raised and received my pastoral theological education in Trinidad, West Indies, and she was from Queens. Nevertheless, I sensed in her a spiritual compatibility, an agreement on fundamental doctrines of the faith and on the meaning of the sacred Scriptures, and within a few short months we were married. I was thirty-three and she was twenty-six, and we were both mature enough and well educated enough to make a wise decision about our future together.

Time proved me right. Wendy Roberts was an extraordinary person. She had a burning desire to share her faith with everyone she met, and she loved everyone—family, friend and stranger alike. When a niece had to be committed to a drug treatment facility, Wendy took in her young son and was a mother to him until his own mother had recovered sufficiently to resume that role. In the exact same way, for the last thirty-one years of her life, she supported children in other parts of the world through World Vision. Most of those children were in Kenya, East Africa, a country she never had the privilege of visiting.

She joined me as a member of the Institutional Crusade for Christ (whose founder and president was Dr. Gwendolyn Washington), and together we did evangelism in prisons, nursing homes, hospitals and on the streets of New York City. Occasionally she also preached in churches. (Mother Washington was present the day we were married and the day of Wendy's graduation to Heaven.)

As a guidance counselor for the NYC Department of Education, Wendy gave up her Saturdays to assist many adults in reaching their career goals in the field of nursing. Even in that secular position, she was a shining light for Jesus.

As a mother, she was unsurpassed. God gave us just one son, but Wendy gave him everything a mother could give, with the goal of preparing him for whatever life held in store for him in the future. In every way, she was an example to him, as she was to others.

When we met in 1976 we were both working on our masters degrees. She got discouraged with her thesis for a time, but as I tell in the book, she eventually finished it and received her title, just in time to apply for a teaching position. She never left things unfinished. That was just not her style.

To me, Wendy Roberts was an angel sent from Heaven. The two of us blended together in all things. Together, we founded a ministry known as Omega Outreach Ministries, Inc., and through this ministry, we gathered and shipped food and Bibles to the Caribbean countries and made missionary trips as well. On these trips, we ministered in prisons, hospitals, nursing homes and out in the villages.

It was on a trip to Antigua that we met Pastor Dexter Lawrence of the Bolands Pentecostal Church. We later went back to work with Pastor Lawrence, and he was the man God used (when he was on a business trip to New York) to administer the Lord's Supper to Wendy for the last time here on Earth.

The thing all of us remember about Wendy Roberts was her peaceful disposition. She was at peace and had a smile on her face—when things were going well and also when things were not going nearly as well. It was heartbreaking for me to see her still displaying that smile, even as she suffered the dreadful affects of cancer and cancer treatment. That sweet face was now terribly swollen, but it still displayed the same smile of peace. Wendy Roberts was the same—from the moment I met her in 1976 until her last breath was taken here on Earth. She taught us all so much.

CONTENTS

Introduction

There is a divine purpose for writing this book. This is not just a book about my wife or her illness or my loss or how we dealt with all of those things; it's about the holiness of Jehovah and His compassion for His people, whom He calls to be sanctified and consecrated. He has also said that we could expect to be afflicted in this world, and that's the part we don't much like.

In the midst of our afflictions, many of us ask the question, "Why me, Lord? Why do I have to face this terrible affliction?" This is the very question that my beloved wife asked after being diagnosed with breast cancer. This book will attempt to answer that common question.

A second objective of the book is to show how our faithful and holy God, our loving heavenly Father, can change the plans of man—even when we consider them to be good. God blesses us with what He, in His wisdom, knows is better for us. He has determined that only His way glorifies His name—to His divine pleasure.

A third objective of the book is to emphasize that holiness is the foundation and fundamental base from which God works with His people. It is His design, through which He blesses His own. The consequence is that we are saved from the pitfalls of life, for we know that a sanctified saint is less likely to move in the flesh, as Samson did. He paid dearly for walking in the spirit of self-deception. God instituted marriage and commands holiness—to bring beauty and happiness to the entire family. In our churches today, for the most part, the emphasis is on good music and lively services, but God still commands the Church to be holy in the twenty-first century. May God help us to better understand His expectation of us today in this regard.

The examples and experiences I cite throughout the book provide an excellent gift and means of ministry support for those who are afflicted or have someone close to them who is afflicted. Sometimes we are at a loss to know what to say when we are ministering to others who are sick or in some other serious affliction. This book can be a source of help in such times. The reading of the selected scriptures can support our objectives, as we seek to meet the challenges of our everyday life. They can build the confidence of the afflicted believer. They will also serve as a help to those who may have to deal with a member of the church who is afflicted or some loved one—a husband, a wife, a brother or some other relative or friend.

In this work, I will not try to peer into the future, to determine what will happen in each individual case—whether there will be healing of ourselves or others based on our intercession in prayer. The focus here is to encourage saints to live each day, saying, with the psalmist, *"This is the day which the* L ORD *hath made; we will re-joice and be glad in it"* (Psalm 118:24), and to trust God for the future.

We must all live in the present. Therefore we should focus on what we can do today so that we will be accounted worthy of eternal life. We must also plan for the future, but with God's purpose and glory in mind.

This book especially deals with cancer. Of all the sicknesses that afflict the human race today, none is so dreaded. This is complicated by the fact that there are many opportunists who choose to use peoples' sicknesses and fears and pressure them for financial gain. This is done through various means, but especially through the media.

The fear that is engendered in this way is a demonic fear, and it can take control of the minds of men and women and even children. Such fear is used to promote medical treatments, foods, vitamins or other natural or organic products that promise to fight cancer. While many of these natural remedies and organic food programs may indeed be effective, we must always be careful not to promise anything that only our Lord can offer. He alone holds the keys of death. He heals or not, according to His will for the moment. Whatever comes our way, as believers we can say, "Thanks be to God, who gives us the victory over fear, the world, the flesh and the devil." And we can live with the outcome, whatever it happens to be.

God's people *must* respond to this current challenge,

because many of His servants are being diagnosed with various forms of cancer today. Far too many of those carry unnecessary mental and emotional burdens as a result. We can help them by using the weapons of spiritual warfare made available to us.

For her part, Wendy fought that good fight of faith with Jesus, her Chief Commander, and the Holy Ghost, the Chief Administrator of the army of God's saints. In the early rounds, she won and received the gift of more years to spend here serving her family and doing God's work on earth. In the final rounds, she lost the battle with cancer, but she won the larger battle in the Spirit.

This book speaks of Wendy Roberts because I knew her intimately and can speak of her case. But you may need to insert your own name in the place of hers or the name of some loved one who suffers. We will all experience affliction of one kind or another in this life, and we need to be ready to face it in a way that pleases our Lord and brings honor to His name.

One thing is certain: whatever we face in life, we are not alone. Never! *Never Alone!*

Daniel Roberts
Springfield Gardens, New York

PROLOGUE

Something was disturbing my rest, calling me back from the depths of sleep. But it was much too early, still very dark outside. I had just finally settled into sleep a couple of hours before, and I desperately needed more of it. What was disturbing me?

I struggled to the surface of consciousness, wanting desperately to know what it was that was troubling my rest and what I could do to stop it. I was very tired. The past days had been so very difficult, emotionally and physically. I'd never faced anything like this before.

I was spending long hours in the hospital by Wendy's side. She needed me more than ever, and I couldn't afford to fail her now. She was the light of my life, my companion of thirty-one years, the mother of my child. Only hours before, I had touched her warm hands and then kissed her warm cheeks and said my good-byes, and I had left her sleeping peacefully in her room.

As I left that night, I noticed that she was breathing without the help of the oxygen, and I was encouraged. It was a good sign, an improvement. Soon my beloved would be strong enough to come home. That would be a welcome day. I needed her by my side.

I had gone straight home and fallen into bed, much too tired to consider eating. Before long I had fallen into a deep sleep. Now something was bringing me back. What was it?

Eventually I realized that the telephone was ringing, and I managed to find it in the dark and answer.

"Is this Mr. Roberts?" the voice on the other end asked.

"Yes," I managed. I knew that voice. It was Wendy's nurse. What could she want at this late hour?

"Mr. Roberts," she said, "I'm sorry to have to tell you this. Wendy Roberts peacefully passed away about 11:00 PM this evening. I'm very sorry."

I froze with the phone still in my hand. It couldn't be! This must be a dream! What was this woman saying? My Wendy, dead? That wasn't possible! I needed her, and she needed me. She couldn't leave me like this.

I'm not sure how long I sat there stunned and unable to answer, unwilling to face the reality of my loss.

"Mr. Roberts," the nurse's voice brought me back to reality, and what she said next cut to the depth of my soul. "We have no refrigeration here, so please make arrangement to have her body removed by the undertakers as soon as possible."

I didn't know what to say to that. What do you say when your wife has become something that suddenly needs to be "removed"? With trembling hands and voice, all I could think of to say was, "Okay."

"Okay!" It struck me, then and now, as a totally inadequate and inappropriate response to what had just happened. It wasn't okay. Nothing was okay. Where was the love of my life? If I had known that she would leave me like this, I would never have left her side. How could I go on living without her? How could I make sense of such a great loss? My heart was broken into a million pieces.

This didn't make any sense. We were both long-standing Christians. We loved the Lord, and He loved us. We not only believed in His salvation; we also believed in His power to heal. So where was God now? Why had He allowed this to happen?

At the moment, all I had was questions, and finding the answers to those questions would take time and prayer. That's what this book is all about. Over time, those answers began to come to me.

For the moment, the news I received that fateful night left me totally devastated. The loss of a longtime mate is considered to be one of the most traumatic experiences known to mankind. We had shared everything, done everything together for so many years. In that moment, I felt so totally alone. But was I really? Never! *Never Alone!*   ✻

And how shall they preach, except they be sent? as it is written, How beautiful are the feet of them that preach the gospel of peace, and bring glad tidings of good things! Romans 10:15

Wendy Roberts teaching the children under the shade of some trees in the village of Johnston's Point on the island of Antigua, during one of our foreign mission trips in 2000

PART I

OUR STORY UNFOLDS

CHAPTER 1

WHY ME, LORD?

*Who shall separate us from the love of Christ? shall
tribulation, or distress, or persecution, or famine, or
nakedness, or peril, or sword? ... Nay, in all these things
we are more than conquerors through him that loved
us.*   Romans 8:35-37

"Why me, Lord?" These were the first words that
came out of Wendy's lips as we arrived home from the
health clinic after the diagnosis of her cancer.

"I have breast cancer." These were words of acknowl-
edgment and acceptance of the stark truth we now faced.

"Why me, Lord?" These were words of pain that only
the Holy Spirit could understand. It is in moments like

this that Jesus is *"touched with the feeling of our infirmities"* (Hebrews 4:15).

But we had a promise from God, as Paul assured the Roman believers in the continuation of the truth of our text verse for this initial chapter:

For I am persuaded, that neither death, nor life, nor angels, nor principalities, nor powers, nor things present, nor things to come, nor height, nor depth, nor any other creature, shall be able to separate us from the love of God, which is in Christ Jesus our Lord.
Romans 8:38-39

This was our only hope in that moment. We embraced each other and, with words of comfort to the woman I loved, I committed myself to do all that I could (with the help of Almighty God) in the midst of this awesome challenge. I would be what God wanted me to be, and I would do what He wanted me to do. The rest was in His hands.

When any believer comes to such a crisis, it is very

> *When any believer comes to such a crisis, it is very important to realize that we cannot change the facts of our affliction!*

important to realize that we cannot change the facts of our affliction. Facts are stubborn things; they don't just go away because they seem unacceptable to us. We have to face them head-on unflinchingly and find the will of God for us in the midst of the reality of our circumstances.

WE'RE ALL CALLED TO BEAR A CROSS

We're all called to bear a cross, but when we take the challenge and enter this walk with God, we have no way of knowing what our particular cross might be. We know one truth; He has promised us all, *"I am with you alway"* (Matthew 28:20). Whatever else happened, I knew that I would never be alone, as much as I might feel alone and lonely at any stage of the journey.

It was not unusual that Wendy should ask the question, "Why me, Lord?" Whenever we are called to bear a burden that may seem to be too great and beyond our human capabilities, in our human weakness, we often ask this question. But should we be surprised when such trials come? Our Lord makes it clear in His Word that we must all go through some tribulation in this life.

Sometimes the tribulation we are called to bear may take the extreme form, actual martyrdom, but more often it will take the form of some less dramatic affliction that we must bear.

There are also times when we will be called upon to bear the afflictions of others. This may require that we spend long hours with them, just being there for them, empathizing with their plight and praying with them to endure. Whatever is required is what we need to do in such moments.

THEY'RE COMMON WORDS

"Why me, Lord?" This is not the only time words like these were spoken from the lips of a servant of the Lord. Moses said the very same thing when he was called to go back and face Pharaoh; he just used different words:

> *Come now therefore, and I will send thee unto Pharaoh, that thou mayest bring forth my people the children of Israel out of Egypt. And Moses said unto God, Who am I, that I should go unto Pharaoh, and that I should bring forth the children of Israel out of Egypt?*
> Exodus 3:10-11

When God called Jeremiah to be a prophet to the nations, he, too, responded in this same very-human way, describing himself as a child and saying assuredly that he could not speak:

> *Before I formed thee in the belly, I knew thee; and before thou camest out of the womb I sanctified thee, and I ordained thee a prophet unto the nations.*
> *Then said I, Ah, Lord GOD! behold, I cannot speak: for I am a child.*
> Jeremiah 1:5-6

In other words, the boldness that was necessary to fulfill Jeremiah's divine mission would require more power than he himself possessed. However, the Lord assured him that this would not be a problem:

> *But the LORD said unto me, Say not, I am a child: for thou shalt go to all that I shall send thee, and whatsoever I command thee thou shalt speak. Be not afraid of their faces: for I am with thee to deliver thee, saith the LORD.* Jeremiah 1:7-8

Although we are reminded that in this life we will have tribulation, we are also assured that in Jesus Christ we will have full peace in the midst of that tribulation. The power of the Holy Spirit will deliver us from all fear, all depression and all oppression and make us able to face whatever life happens to throw our way.

"GOD DOESN'T CARE!"

When we are afflicted, many mental attacks are then launched against us by the enemy. Thank God that we know his devices. Satan tries to tell us that God has abandoned us, that He doesn't love us any more and that He doesn't even care that we're suffering. The tempter may say things like, "If you're a child of God and He loves you, then why are you in such a pitiful condition? Just look at yourself." The answer to that lie is very simply: "There is no way the love of Jesus for me can be denied. He went to the cross for me. What could possibly demonstrate more the fact that He loves me and He cares about my suffering."

NEVER ALONE!

Isaiah was used to declare it:

But now, saith the LORD that created thee, O Jacob, and he that formed thee, O Israel, Fear not: for I have redeemed thee, I have called thee by thy name; thou art mine. When thou passest through the waters, I will be with thee; and through the rivers, they shall not overflow thee: when thou walkest through the fire, thou shalt not be burned: neither shall the flame kindle upon thee. For I am the LORD thy God, the Holy One of Israel, thy Savior.   Isaiah 43:1-3

That says it all. Whatever comes our way, God and His love for us does not change. Ever! He is there with us. We are *Never Alone!*

THE COURAGE TO ACKNOWLEDGE SUFFERING

When faced with cancer or some other such serious affliction, we need courage to acknowledge the thing that has come upon us. Cancer is the most unwelcome word in the English language today and has become the battleground where many have fought and lost. But although we may sometimes lose in the physical, we are always victorious in the Spirit, and that is far better.

This is exactly what the apostle Paul was intent on conveying through the Holy Spirit, when he wrote to the members of the early Corinthian church:

But we have this treasure in earthen vessels, that the excellency of the power may be in God, and not of us.

We are troubled on every side, yet not distressed; we are perplexed, but not in despair; persecuted, but not forsaken; cast down, but not destroyed.

2 Corinthians 4:7-9

Have the courage to acknowledge your own trial, knowing that you can overcome it in Christ.

THE COURAGE NOT TO FORSAKE THE AFFLICTED

The challenge for every child of the living God today is not to forsake those brothers and sisters who are currently suffering affliction. We have a commandment to obey. Our Lord declared:

By this shall all men know that you are my disciples, if ye have love one to another.

John 13:35

When faced with cancer or some other such serious affliction, we need courage to acknowledge the thing that has come upon us!

Certainly such love is not to be exercised only in good times, but also when those we are called to love find themselves afflicted. Sadly, when our friends need us most, we often forsake them, considering that

27

they are somehow not spiritual enough because of what has befallen them. This is a serious error.

A Pastor's Comfort with Truth and Love

The first time Wendy was diagnosed with cancer, we thought we knew what to do. God is the Healer, so we began to believe Him for her healing. A pastor and friend came to visit us and pray with us. That day he made a statement that remains forever true to the Word of God and to His Spirit. We could pray, and God would answer, but He might choose to answer in one of two ways. He could heal Wendy, or He could choose to give her grace to bear up under her trial. The choice was not ours, but God's alone.

Since our pastor did not know the future or the perfect will of God in this particular matter, we prayed together for God's mercy and, by faith, opened our hearts to know what He had ordained in this particular situation. We were delighted when God answered our prayers, displaying His mercy by healing Wendy and giving her three more years to enjoy life here on earth.

Now What?

But now the cancer was back. First it came as breast cancer, but now it was a brain tumor. What were we to do? We were in agreement that if God had done it once, then He could do it again. So we began to pray in the same way. But, as before, the choice would be His, not ours. The authority to heal is God's alone, the will to heal is also His, and if He chooses not to heal, then we know that His grace is sufficient for any trial. And whatever God chooses to do in such a situation, we can rest assured in His promise:

And we know that all things work together for good to them that love God, to them who are the called according to his purpose. Romans 8:28

We were on a new adventure with God, and what the outcome was to be we didn't yet know. What we did know was that we would never be alone. Never! *Never Alone!* ✻

CHAPTER 2

A NIGHT TO REMEMBER

Surely, he shall not be moved for ever: the righteous shall be in everlasting remembrance. He shall not be afraid of evil tidings: his heart is fixed, trusting in the LORD. His heart is established, he shall not be afraid.

Psalm 112:6-8

Memory is a gift from God. He causes us to remember. In His creative wisdom, He ordained the mystery of memory, even as He created man for His divine purposes. God has blessed us with the awesome capacity to recall from the millions of pieces of information stored in the memory bank of our brains and intellect, so that we can bring to mind what He has done for us and give Him thanks for His faithfulness. Thanks be to God for this wonderful blessing! Yes, there are negative memories, as well, and we'll get to that presently. God knows how to deal with those too.

THE DANGER OF FORGETTING GOD

We understand, through the records of God's Word, the Bible, that when God's people remember Him and His mighty acts and the power to deliver and save them from evil and destruction, they usually trust Him and love Him and believe Him for what He is able to do. But when God's people forget Him and the testimonies of His loving kindness, they run the risk of committing acts of evil, and the spirit of unbelief soon possesses them. The psalmist declared:

> *They soon forgat his works; they waited not for his counsel: but lusted exceedingly in the wilderness, and tempted God in the desert. And he gave them their request; but sent leaness into their soul.*
>
> Psalm 106:13-15

We cannot afford to forget God.

GOD ALWAYS REMEMBERS AND WE MUST TOO

God remembers to bless us, and if He remembers to bless us, it is only natural that we, who are His children, should remember Him as well and that we should be thankful to Him and willing to become a blessing to others. God desires to bless us, and He remembers us, because He is totally faithful. His holiness and steadfast love demand that His righteous and divine nature work in harmony with His justice:

> *For he remembered his holy promise, and Abraham his servant. And he brought forth his people with joy, and his chosen with gladness: and gave them the lands of the heathen: and they inherited the labour of the people.*
>
> Psalm 105:42-44

When we fail to remember the goodness and faithfulness of God, we become little more than beasts. Therefore we cannot afford to forget. We must not forget God, and we must not forget the selfless acts of others who have blessed us.

> *God remembers to bless us, and ... it is only natural that we, who are His children, should remember Him as well!*

Remembering the Good Things Done for Us

For instance, we cannot afford to forget the acts of those who took care of us when we were young. If we forget the deeds and sacrifices of our parents and others, from whom we have received loving kindness in various ways, we become ungrateful and unthankful and also unholy and unmerciful. Here are a list of sins of the heart found in those who forget, and they're all found in a single chapter of the Bible—Psalm 106. It includes sins against God and against others:

1. Verse 14 (*"[They] lusted exceedingly."*)
2. Verse 15 (They trusted in themselves.)
3. Verse 16 (*"They envied Moses."*)
4. Verse 19 (They became idolaters.)
5. Verse 28 (They became defiled and unclean.)
6. Verse 29 (They had evil intentions.)
7. Verse 38 (*"[They] shed innocent blood,"* or murdered.)
8. Verse 38 (They offered human sacrifices.)
9. Verse 38 (They polluted the land with blood.)

It never pays to forget God and His goodness.

A Night I Will Always Remember

Unfortunately, as we noted earlier, not all memories are good. We all seem to have a particular day or night that stands out in our memories for all time. It is sometimes because it's a bad memory, one that has touched some deep emotions.

On my own most memorable night, I touched the warm hands of God's servant and kissed her warm cheeks, said good-bye and left her sleeping peacefully in the clinic. I had no idea that it would be the last time I saw her, and that within a few hours, she would be gone from us forever. If I had known that, I'm sure I would have lingered even longer, wanting to feel the warmth of her tender hands as long as possible.

I had ministered to her with Bible reading and prayer for several hours that historic evening, Thursday, the 16th day of the month of August, 2007. Then, after speaking to her the words the Holy Spirit gave me, I decided that it was time for me to leave for the night and get some rest. Tomorrow was another day, and her sister and other friends would be coming to see her.

It was about nine o'clock when I left for home. Very tired, I went right to bed without eating. It was too late to eat, and soon I fell fast asleep.

I must have been sleeping for about two hours when the phone woke me. The voice on the other end was Wendy's nurse. "Mr. Roberts," she said, "Wendy Roberts peacefully passed away about 11 PM this evening. I'm sorry."

That was when I froze with the phone in my hand, and when all I could say in response to this tragic news was "Okay."

But, again, it wasn't okay. I needed help. I couldn't think. What did I need to do? I was so alone in that moment.

Trembling, I called my brother in the Bronx and told him and received his words of comfort, and then I called her sister, with whom she had a very close relationship. We were to have met the next day and gone together to see her. Now those plans had been changed. What was I to do now? My world had suddenly come crashing down!

NOT WITHOUT HOPE

In all of this, I was not without hope. I knew the scriptures:

> *I desperately needed, in that moment, a song in my heart, a song in the night!*

That we through patience and comfort of the scriptures might have hope. Now the God of hope fill you with all joy and peace in believing, that ye may abound in hope, through the power of the Holy Ghost.
Romans 15:4 and 13

Still, I desperately needed, in that moment, a song in my heart, a song in the night. As believers, we often sing praises to God, but it's different when we can find comfort even in the night seasons.

The emotions of such a night can be so unforgiving and ruthless. It would be wise for any of us to keep an inventory of songs in our hearts just for the times when we may need them. Sing one of those songs, and see how deliverance will come to your soul. Such a song can bring total refreshing. Here's an old one that spoke to me that night:

Tell it to Jesus

Are you weary, are you heavy hearted?
Tell it to Jesus, Tell it to Jesus!
Are you grieving over joys departed?
Tell it to Jesus alone.

Chorus:
Tell it to Jesus, Tell it to Jesus.
He is a friend that's well known.
You've no other such a friend or brother;
Tell it to Jesus alone.

Do the tears flow down your cheeks unbidden?
Tell it to Jesus, Tell it to Jesus.
Have you sins that to men's eyes are hidden?
Tell it to Jesus alone.

Telling Jesus what I was feeling and experiencing seemed to be my only option at the moment, but it was the right thing to do. He understood and comforted me.

The Grimmest Task

The grimmest task I had to face that night was to go to the basement, where our son was still up, even then playing his guitar and singing, and tell him we had just lost his mother. In the end, I couldn't bring myself to do it. "Let him enjoy one more night of happiness," I reasoned, "before entering into an undetermined period of grief and loneliness and tears. Don't rob him of a good night's sleep. He'll need it to face this trial." The next day I would get his aunt to gently share the news with him.

Right then I had my own grief to deal with. How could I go on living without my Wendy? Why would God take a woman as wonderful as she was from the earth? Didn't we all need her? Didn't she serve a useful purpose here for His Kingdom? In the end, I came to realize that even when God takes away someone so righteous, He still has a divine purpose for it. And who are we to question the sovereignty of God?

How Can We Know?

How can we know that God's will is being done when a saint is taken from us? Sometimes we hear someone say that this person should have changed his or her diet or they should have gone to a healing and deliverance minister and been prayed for. If that's the case, then did God fail to give them divine direction so that they could be positioned in the right place at the right time to receive their healing and deliverance? Surely not! There is a lot that we cannot know for sure, but one thing we do know. He who is faithful never fails. If there has been a failure, it must have been on our part, not His.

God would never take a righteous man out of this world simply because he had made a mistake in His service to the King, and neither would He allow some catastrophe to shorten the days He has ordained for that saint to fulfill his mission here for the Master's glory. The future of the righteous is in the hands of Almighty God. Therefore we must walk in Gospel obedience and leave the rest to Him.

God said through Isaiah:

The righteous perisheth, and no man layeth it to heart: and merciful men are taken away, none considering that the righteous is taken away from the evil to come.
                                        Isaiah 57:1

I was so alone that night. Or was I? Never! *Never Alone!*   ✳

CHAPTER 3

CANCER WAS NO MATCH FOR A CONSECRATED WOMAN

When thou passest through the waters, I will be with thee; and through the rivers, they shall not overflow thee: when thou walkest through the fire, thou shalt not be burned; neither shall the flame kindle upon thee.

Isaiah 43:2

When cancer attacks with a vengeance, the Holy Spirit responds with supernatural power. The Scriptures declare: *"The LORD hath his way in the whirlwind"* (Nahum 1:3). Our afflictions seem to come like a whirlwind, but the Prince of Peace shelters and comforts us in those moments. For the consecrated saint of God, therefore, there is peace.

MANY BECOME ANGRY

This is not the case with many. When cancer strikes them, they become angry and begin to lash out, blaming anyone they can for their troubles. It's the fault of farmers and what they spray on their crops. It's the fault of food manufacturers and processors and the chemicals they insert into their foods to preserve them longer.

> *When cancer strikes them, they become angry and begin to lash out, blaming anyone they can for their troubles!*

Such anger helps no one. We all know that evil men, in cooperation with the devil, have been and continue to be the cause of much of the suffering in our world. Without a doubt, man is guilty of destroying the earth, from which we must derive all that is needed for our sustenance, and that directly affects our health. Still, despite all the bad news of the day (and this has been true in every generation), we believers have hope and joy. God is still in control.

Paul wrote the Thessalonians:

Rejoice evermore. Pray without ceasing. In every thing give thanks: for this is the will of God in Christ Jesus concerning you. 1 Thessalonians 5:16-18

42

"Evermore!" "In everything!" That says it all.

The afflicted believer has many promises from God and can plan for a glorious future. God's intent is for all of His children to have *"life"* and have it *"more abundantly"* (John 10:10). Even those who are afflicted with cancer can often go on to live a very productive life. Every saint can still reach out to others, and there are always places to go and things to do. All the believer can do under the circumstances is to strive to be their best in terrible circumstances and to trust God for the rest.

When Wendy was struck with cancer, together God gave us the determination to travel and testify to His goodness. We would let His will be accomplished. He does all things well, and we were sure that we could trust Him.

MY WAYS ARE NOT YOUR WAYS

Soon the Lord would tell us that we could retire from our secular jobs and have more time to serve Him. Although His plan for our future was in the New York City area, we only understood this in time. Our own desire was to live in Florida, and we tried it for a time. In the end, we moved back to New York.

This is often the way God deals with us. At some point, we come to understand that the circumstances of our life have brought us into God's perfect will, but we don't always understand it before looking back. Looking back on past decisions, we can then see how God has brought us to where we are.

That message now came to us loud and clear. It has always been this way with those whom Christ calls to be His disciples:

For my thoughts are not your thoughts, neither are your ways my ways, saith the LORD. For as the heavens are higher than the earth, so are my ways higher than your ways, and my thoughts than your thoughts.
Isaiah 55:8-9

WHAT DO YOU DO WHEN CANCER RETURNS?

Within six weeks of our return to New York, it was revealed that the cancer had returned. This was not good news in any sense of the word, but we still had to praise God. He had demonstrated that He was God, by keeping the cancer under control for the past three years. The future was in His hands. He was a great and loving Father who did all things well, according to His purposes. How could we not trust Him?

And that's what we did. Along with whatever medications Wendy's doctors prescribed, we trusted God. We trusted Him for His mercy and for His healing power.

THIS TIME, THE OUTCOME WAS DIFFERENT

This time, the outcome was different, and over the next two years, my role changed. My primary responsibility was now caring for our home and serving my increasingly ailing wife. As her condition worsened, God gave me added grace.

Unlike some cancer sufferers, Wendy did not have severe pain. Thank God for that. She just didn't feel good, and she experienced serious weakness. God was preparing us for an experience of a lifetime. When it came, we would make it through each day only by the miraculous working of His Holy Spirit.

Through it all, He gave us joy:

Speaking to yourselves in psalms and hymns and spiritual songs, singing and making melody in your heart to the Lord; giving thanks always for all things unto God and the Father in the name of our Lord Jesus Christ.   Ephesians 5:19-20

As Wendy's condition now grew from not so good, to bad and then to worse, we were not afraid. We had God's promise:

He shall cover thee with his feathers, and under his wings shalt thou trust: his truth shall be thy shield and buckler. Thou shalt not be afraid for the terror by night; nor for the arrow that flieth by day.
                                                   Psalm 91:4-5

PREPARING FOR BETTER DAYS

How could we prepare for better days when we saw the increasingly devastating effects of this terrible sick-

45

ness? All consecrated saints have one thing in common in such times. We have the abiding presence of Jesus, who said that He would never leave us, nor forsake us. Those comforting words were given so that we could know there was always Someone nearby who understood what we were going through. He feels our pain:

> *For we have not an high priest which cannot be touched with the feeling of our infirmities; but was in all points tempted like as we are, yet without sin.*
> Hebrews 4:15

We have a destiny, and we are conquerors in all things—no matter what our current situation may be. We are equipped with the spiritual weapons we need to overcome our principle enemy—fear of the unknown.

Just think of the ways Satan tries to bring fear into our hearts, and yet we are victorious in it all, *"more than conquerors"*:

> *Nay, in all these things we are more than conquerors through him that loved us. For I am persuaded, that neither death, nor life, nor angels, nor principalities, nor powers, nor things present, nor things to come, nor height, nor depth, nor any other creature, shall be able to separate us from the love of God, which is in Christ Jesus our Lord.* Romans 8:37-39

Fear was and is our number one enemy, but Jesus conquered him through His death, His victory of the cross and His resurrection.

Drawing on Our Reflections

Each of us, in difficult times, must draw on our good years, the ministry, the labor for God, the fruits that have been borne. The fruits of our labors, our works, then become our consolation, and we draw from all the wonderful service we've had pleasure in, as we worked for and with the King of Kings. His final commendation is our joy and will be our joy forever.

In a later chapter, "Awaiting Our Own 'Well Done,' " I will expand on this wonderful topic of our Lord's words spoken as His saints come to stand before Him. It is a future we all have to look forward to.

In the meantime, as our trial grew more grim, were we alone? Never! *Never Alone!*   ✳

CHAPTER 4

FEAR WAS ALSO NO MATCH FOR HER

Forasmuch then as the children are partakers of flesh and blood, he also himself likewise took part of the same; that through death he might destroy him that had the power of death, that is, the devil; and deliver them who through fear of death were all their lifetime subject to bondage. Hebrews 2:14-15

The enemy launched his attacks on Wendy's spirit many times, but she remained steadfast, until he came with the spirit of fear, and then the battle became extremely intense. This battle lasted for only about two days, but during that time, I could not help her. The devil was attacking her mind, and I had no way of getting inside there.

NEVER ALONE!

THE COMFORTER WAS NEAR

Thanks be to God for the work of the Holy Spirit (whom, Jesus said, would come to be our *"Comforter"* (John 14:16). Our Helper was there. He came, and as He promised, was with us to the end. How we would have made it without Him I cannot say. It was an extremely difficult time. As much as I would have liked it to be different, it was the Lord's battle, and when that is the case, there will always be victory.

My prayers over this two-year period had been for the nurturing and strengthening of our inner man and for us to be filled with the Holy Spirit, so that we could prepare for the increasing battle. If you don't understand that now, you will at some point. Your time will come. Walk close to God, and let Him teach you how to engage in real spiritual warfare when it comes.

The writer of the Hebrews gives us the hope and assurance that He who conquered death and fear for Himself is also able to deliver us when the enemy comes to us in our personal Garden of Gethsemane:

For in that he himself hath suffered being tempted, he is able to succour [help] them that are tempted.

Hebrews 2:18

Far too many of us have been kept in slavery because of fear, but when Jesus came, He delivered us from all such fear and, being delivered, we can say with the apostle Paul:

O death, where is thy sting? O grave, where is thy victory?

1 Corinthians 15:55

This simply means that the sting of death has been disarmed, and the victory that the grave had is now changed to defeat (when it comes to those who are in Christ). It was because of this that Stephen, as he fell asleep in Christ, being stoned, was victorious. He was not defeated in death; he triumphed that day.

The greater context of this passage says this:

So when this corruptible shall have put on incorruption, and this mortal shall have put on immortality, then shall be brought to pass the saying that is written,... O death, where is thy sting? O grave, where is thy victory? The sting of death is sin; and the strength of sin is the law. But thanks be to God, which giveth us the victory through our Lord Jesus Christ.

1 Corinthians 15:54-57

The sting of death has been disarmed, and the victory that the grave had is now changed to defeat (when it comes to those who are in Christ)!

MISDIRECTED FOCUS

The reason fear is often able to grip our minds is that, for some reason, our focus becomes misdirected. That's the physical part. Emotionally, spirits seek to altar our thoughts of faith and confidence in the truth. When fear comes in, it brings with it doubts concerning the truth.

When you consider the standard strategies of the wicked one, it's very easy to see his *modus operandi* in this regard. He came to Jesus to tempt Him at the beginning of His ministry, when He was weak from fasting and praying in the wilderness. Satan lost the battle on that occasion, so he left Jesus for a season, but he returned when Jesus was again physically weak, sweating drops of blood in the agony of His conflict in the Garden of Gethsemane, and he tried again to subvert Jesus' faith. That's just the way the devil operates.

We know that the enemy's overall goal is to derail our faith in the hope of eternal life and our confidence in the resurrection of Jesus Christ from the dead. That's the point of his last stand with every believer. God was very good to us in that He allowed us to have two years head start on the enemy. Our preparation for this battle was intense during those two years. Our God went on the offensive, to gain a victory for His saints.

THE PSALMIST DAVID AND HIS FEARS

The psalmist David handled the fears that attacked him with the Word of God. Those fears seemed to come to him periodically, not consistently and continuously. This may have been in unguarded moments. So guard your spirit and look out for those moments when it seems that there is nothing particular on your mind. David said:

What time I am afraid, I will trust in thee. In God I will praise his word, in God I have put my trust; I will not fear what flesh can do unto me.   Psalm 56:3-4

Fear comes also from an uncertainty of the future. And fear increases when there is no strength to trust and hope, and when, in times of conflict, there is no defense and no deliverer. In such a time, our questions are answered by Jehovah:

He that planted the ear, shall he not hear? he that formed the eye, shall he not see? He that chastiseth the heathen, shall he not correct? he that teacheth man knowledge, shall not he know?   Psalm 94:9-10

In this, God is simply saying to us, "I know, and I care about your fears, and you will go through this victoriously." That's enough for me.

Job Handled His Fears

Sickness and death suddenly surrounded Job, just when he was experiencing the best years of his life in the area of peace and prosperity. The next thing Job knew, trouble had come without warning:

NEVER ALONE!

For the thing which I greatly feared is come upon me, and that which I was afraid of is come unto me. I was not in safety, neither had I rest, neither was I quiet; yet trouble came.　　　　Job 3:25-26

But Job's hope stood against his fear and enabled him to overcome:

> *Job's hope stood against his fear and enabled him to overcome!*

For I know that my redeemer liveth, and that he shall stand at the latter day ... and though after my skin worms destroy this body, yet in my flesh shall I see God: whom I shall see for myself, and mine eyes shall behold, and not another.　　　Job 19:25-27

Today we remember Job as a man who overcame severe hardship and went on to prosper.

JOHN THE BAPTIST AND HIS FEARS

John the Baptist had a fear of deception, but he used wisdom to handle that temptation, by going directly to the spiritual Source of all knowledge and getting the answer directly from Christ:

And John calling unto him two of his disciples sent them to Jesus, saying, Art thou he that should come? or look

*we for another? When the men were come unto him,
they said, John Baptist hath sent us unto thee, saying,
Art thou he that should come? or look we for another?
And in that same hour he cured many of their infirmities and plagues, and of evil spirits; and unto many
that were blind he gave sight. Then Jesus answering
said unto them, Go your way, and tell John what things
ye have seen and heard; how that the blind see, ... the
deaf hear, the dead are raised, to the poor the gospel is
preached.* Luke 7:19-22

John wanted to be sure that the voice he had heard on
the banks of the river Jordan was indeed the voice of God
and not of another. He wanted to be sure that the testimony he made that very day of the Messiah was true and
not mistaken. He wanted to get the facts straight one last
time. He was about to lose his life for the sake of the Gospel, and the last thing anyone wants is to die without the
hope of eternal life. John got his answer and was able to
die in peace and assurance.

THIS SAME WEAPON WAS USED AGAINST JESUS

The attack against Jesus in the Garden of Gethsemane was with this same weapon of fear. The cross that
we must all bear one day is the moment in our lives
when the devil uses fear as his greatest temptation.

With Jesus, the devil failed miserably, but Jesus
warned the disciples to pray, lest they be found wanting
in their time of temptation:

NEVER ALONE!

And when he was at the place, he said unto them,
Pray that ye enter not into temptation.
And he said unto them, Why sleep ye? rise and pray,
lest ye enter into temptation.   Luke 22:40 and 46

Your day is coming. Be ready!

ENCOURAGE YOURSELVES

The Word of God is a weapon for warfare that we must use in times such as these. We can cling to that Word, and we can speak it, and, in so doing, we can encourage ourselves in the Lord. This is the work of the Holy Spirit who dwells inside the soul of every believer, every man, woman, boy or girl who has been born again. The Spirit abiding in us is the promise that Jesus fulfilled for us, through His resurrection and ascension.

Do you have a song that you can sing in such a difficult time as this? Here are the words of a song that Wendy sometimes sang to bring the joy of the Lord to deliver her mind from nagging doubts and fears. It worked because, *"The joy of the LORD is your strength"* (Nehemiah 8:10):

BEFORE THE THRONE

Before the throne of God above
I have a strong and perfect plea,
A great High Priest whose name is Love,
Who ever lives and pleads for me.

My name is written in His heart.
I know that while in Heaven He stands,
No tongue can bid me thence depart.
No tongue can bid me thence depart.

When Satan tempts me to despair
And tells me of the guilt within,
Upward I look and see Him there,
Who made an end to all my sins.
Because the sinless Savior died,
My sinful soul is counted free.
For God, the just is satisfied,
To look on Him and pardon me,
To Look on Him and pardon me.

Behold Him there, the risen Lamb,
My perfect, spotless righteousness,
The great unchangeable I AM,
The King of glory and of grace.
One with Himself I cannot die.
My soul is purchased with His blood.
My life is hid with Christ on high,
With Christ my Savior and my God,
With Christ my Savior and my God.

—Charite L. Bancroft (1891-1892)

In many of our modernday churches, the trend is away from song books, and there are, therefore, few songs to truly remember. Because the congregational singing requires an overhead projector, there is no way to sing many of the same songs at home. One of the treasured traditions of the past was to gather our families at home and, together with them, to sing songs of praise to God. This tradition is too good to lose. Therefore, every home needs some old-fashioned hymnals and Gospel song books.

Learn some hymns for your own use in the future and some of the biblical spiritual songs. Memorize them. You'll need them in the times to come to encourage your heart, just as Paul and Silas did when they were imprisoned for their faith. There, in that small jail cell, they had no drums, guitars or pianos. They sang out of their hearts to God.

What did Paul and his companion in faith sing? Possibly the psalms. What would you do if you were imprisoned in some foreign country and you had no Bible, no song books and no other type of Christian reading material? Think of the stress that would cause and the depression that would try to take hold of your mind.

Get ready for any eventuality. Do whatever you need to do to send the evil one fleeing and to keep your faith strong to overcome all fear.

Were we alone? Never! *Never Alone!* ✳

CHAPTER 5

RETIREMENT AND OUR ALTERED PLANS

The steps of a good man are ordered by the LORD: and he delighteth in his way.   Psalm 37:23

Somehow the Father, in His sovereign and providential will, moved upon my mind to consider early retirement. There were several things that brought me to this decision.

For one, I kept thinking how much more I could do for God in His service if I were free of my teaching responsibilities. But there was another consideration. I was suffering severe pain as I walked, the result, I was told, of a degenerating disk in my spine. I needed some time to relax and let that mend.

It actually may have been more this latter cause that made me consider giving up my quest for earthly treasure. My salary was very attractive, and yet I decided to obey the Lord and retire. The Lord's will must always have priority in the lives of His people, since He is Lord, and that means that He rules.

CAREFUL CONSIDERATION

> *The circumstances of life often move us in God's direction!*

This move was not without careful consideration. I was about to give up something that most people consider to be the most precious and valuable. The apostle Paul, however, saw it as it really was. He called it *"dung"*:

But what things were gain to me, those I counted loss for Christ. Yea doubtless, and I count all things but loss for the excellency of the knowledge of Christ Jesus my Lord: for whom I have suffered the loss of all things, and do count them but dung, that I may win Christ.

Philippians 3:7-8

My decision to retire coincided perfectly with Wendy's forced retirement. God can move upon our will to do what we need to do and not what we want to do.

THE CIRCUMSTANCES OF LIFE OFTEN
MOVE US IN GOD'S DIRECTION

It is in this way that the circumstances of life often move us in God's direction. What results is His will and not our own. And one of those circumstances that move us God's way is sickness.

Serious sickness often causes us to make decisions which we would not otherwise have made, if we were enjoying good health. Wendy was much too young to retire, but she now had no choice in the matter. It was decided for her.

Many saints who seek to walk in God's divine will are constantly looking for a way to escape the world of secular work so that they can walk in faith, in service to Christ. And there's nothing wrong with that. But we must walk by the leading of the Holy Spirit, looking for divine revelation to show us when and how to make the necessary move, for which there is no turning back. As our theme verse for this chapter notes: *"The steps of a good man are ordered by the LORD: and he delighteth in his way"* (Psalm 37:23).

THE RIGHTEOUS WILL NEVER BE FORSAKEN

In such moments, we wonder what may happen if our plan is somehow a mistake, but we must remember that God makes no mistakes. He, the Eternal One, never enters into any risky business. Thank God that He is God, and He is the Faithful One who stands solidly behind His word.

The call and move of the Holy Spirit is stronger than what we see from the natural perspective. Our financial and protection plans for our future medical and basic necessities can never prepare us for the unseen future.

As saints of God, when we understand His still, small voice and still cannot determine the unseen future, we depend on what He has promised and know that He will intervene when we need Him. We realize that whatever we need for the future will require the supernatural providence of God, but that's not a problem. He gives us His blessed assurance.

When God makes it impossible for us to go the way we had planned, we come to the experience Paul had as he journeyed on the road to Damascus. There his life was forcibly turned around. As David said:

God is my strength and power: And he maketh my way perfect. 2 Samuel 22:33

We would soon experience just that. In such moments, we must hear God saying to us, *"Your ways are not my ways":*

For my thoughts are not your thoughts, neither are your ways my ways, saith the LORD. For as the heavens are higher than the earth, so are my ways higher than your ways, and my thoughts than your thoughts. Isaiah 55:8-9

An educational attainment could never be used to determine a future or to devise a plan that was acceptable to God. He alone is the one who determines what path we must take for His divine pleasure.

All too often we measure our abilities by the degrees we have earned, but they cannot be taken into consideration for decision-making. Any decision-making which stands apart from the wisdom of God is doomed to failure.

What a Great Plan We Had!

What a great plan we had! Everything seemed to fit. We would retire from our current positions and move to Florida. We had already bought and paid for a house there, and it was fully furnished. We could work as volunteer teachers at a private Christian school and also work with a local pastor and his congregation in a new church in Tampa. From Florida, we would continue to collect and pack barrels of food to send to churches in the Caribbean to distribute to their poor.

It all looked good to us, but our good is never God's good unless and until He embraces it and approves it. When this doesn't happen (as in this case), we must bow to His wishes, saying, "The will of the Lord be done." There's no need to condemn ourselves in such cases, but we do need to repent and seek the plan God has had for us since the foundation of the world. This requires waiting before Him in prayer.

Was Moving to Florida God's Will?

God allowed us to spend some weeks in that beautiful house, enjoying the scenery of the nearby lake, but He knew that we would not be staying there permanently as we had planned. It took us a while to realize it, and that's why it's so important for us to know the mind of Christ and have the leading of the Holy Ghost. Thank God He cares.

Was it all a bad idea? Not really! But God had a better plan, and it was through His plan that His glory would be revealed.

Can God get glory out of what we plan? Of course, He can, but sometimes His plans are different.

God Uses Our Weaknesses to Work Out His Eternal Plan

Divine order often causes us to do things in our lives, not because we want to, but because we need to. Even, because we *have* to. Consider the case of Moses.

Moses was the chosen manchild God had seen before the foundations of the world and destined to set His people free. Before he got there, however, through his own anger, Moses murdered an Egyptian, and because of it, became a fugitive from Egyptian justice. But God used that very situation to make his servant do what he would never have wanted to do otherwise. It was his flight from Pharaoh's officials that brought him right where God wanted him.

God is not *"the author of confusion"* (1 Corinthians 14:33), and He's also not a murderer. It's the devil who's a murderer and has been from the beginning. Still, in His sovereign will and counsel, God chose to use Moses so that he could never glory in any of his own achievements. He was perfect for leading the children of Israel out of bondage.

When Moses recognized the majesty and glory of God's excellence, he knew that God was so holy that he couldn't ever compare himself with Jehovah. This realization caused him to fear (respect) God:

> *(For they could not endure that which was commanded, And if so much as a beast touch the mountain, it shall be stoned, or thrust through with a dart: and so terrible was the sight, that Moses said, I exceedingly fear and quake.)*
> Hebrews 12:20-21

Divine order often causes us to do things in our lives, not because we want to, but because we need to!

We have a great advantage over Moses, for we now live on the other side of Calvary and can appreciate all that Jesus did for us there. We have the privilege of approaching the presence of God through the blood of the sacrificial Lamb.

The point is that God used it all for His glory. Were we alone in our mistaken move to Florida and our subsequent return to New York? Never! *Never Alone!*   ✳

Chapter 6

Why Some Are Healed and Others Are Not

And when he was come to the temple, the chief priests and the elders of the people came unto him as he was teaching, and said, By what authority doest thou these things? and who gave thee this authority?

Matthew 21:23

Jesus answered the question, but not to these particular men and not right then and there. He did it only to His own disciples and at a place and time of His own choosing.

When these religious leaders asked this question, *"Who gave thee this authority?"* they were not sincerely looking for truth, only trying to find a way to accuse

Jesus. However, it's a good question. Where does the authority to heal come from?

The power we receive to become sons of God through the work of salvation is not the same as the power and authority needed to heal. The Scriptures make it clear that although the apostles were born again and filled with the Holy Spirit, that did not qualify them to make things happen as they willed. They needed God's authority specifically for the working of miracles, for healing and for deliverance. The power of God must be *"present to heal"* (Luke 5:17).

Use God's Words

It is also necessary that the words we speak on such occasions be given to us by the Holy Spirit Himself. In absolutely everything, God is in control, and He will not share His glory with anyone.

This was the problem Moses had one day when he spoke out of his flesh about the water the children of Israel needed. This angered God and resulted in Moses losing the right to enter the Promised Land. When we speak, we must be careful to speak God's words spoken under His authority. In such moments, the words that proceed out of our mouths must never be influenced by the flesh.

But how merciful is our God? He still gave the children of Israel their needed water. Moses was their earthly leader, but God Himself was their Shepherd. He fed and cared for them, just as a shepherd feeds and cares for his sheep.

This need to speak God's words under His authority is one of the problems facing many Christian pastors and leaders today. God can guarantee eternal life through the work of the cross, but can we, then, ask for healing through His name and always receive deliverance without delay? Is healing a guaranteed blessing, as is salvation? The answer is to be found here in the words of Christ when He finally did respond to the question of the religious leaders. We'll get to that shortly.

PRIDE AND COMPASSION

After Wendy died, several people asked why, after all the praying and fasting we had done, had she not been healed. To me, the answer was simple. When God gives the authority, there will be healing—even though the instrument He uses employs his or her own words. God has promised healing and He always honors His promises. The thing that is very troubling to me is that when we pray, the words we speak may give a false hope and assurance to the afflicted, and what we say may

It is also necessary that the words we speak on such occasions be given to us by the Holy Spirit Himself!

69

never come to pass. This is a serious matter that requires more careful attention.

At one point, the disciples were unable to help a man who brought his son to them. This was the man who confessed his lack of faith to Jesus:

And straightway the father of the child cried out, and said with tears, Lord, I believe; help thou mine unbelief.
                                                          Mark 9:24

The apostles had not been able to help him because they had a conflict between pride and compassion. Pride seeks glory without sacrifice, but compassion seeks to suffer for the deliverance of others.

I believe that we should accept the fact that God, our heavenly Father, is always moved by the bitterness of our tears and the anguish of our souls. When this child's father cried from the depths of his soul, the Lord was moved with compassion to help his unbelief and granted him his request for healing.

The Sovereign Will of God Always Determines the Outcome

Of course, the sovereign will of God will always determine the final outcome. It's not because we cry with bitter tears that we will receive the petition we ask of Him. The prophet Samuel, for instance, prayed and cried all night for the life of Saul and his restoration as king over Israel, and yet God did not grant that request. Saul had committed the sin of rebellion, and his heart had been turned to an unacceptable apostate condition. Therefore, there was no repentance or forgiveness for him, only irreversible destruction:

> *Then came the word of the LORD unto Samuel, saying, It repenteth me that I have set up Saul to be king: for he is turned back from following me, and hath not performed my commandments. And it grieved Samuel; and he cried unto the LORD all night.*
>
> 1 Samuel 15:10-11

My prayer is that God will give those who are ministering to the afflicted the wisdom to seek His face, so that they can be led in prayer for each individual believer. Just going from one to the other, declaring the same thing over each one is unacceptable. The afflicted need to know the will of God for their particular case with all understanding and confidence.

THE POWER AND AUTHORITY

Without power and authority nothing can be accomplished. This is true in the natural, as well as the spiritual. Every police officer must be given both power and authority to perform an assigned task. If, for instance, officers are facing the participants of an unruly protest march, they must simply stand there until they are given authority to do something more. They cannot act without authorization.

71

There are policemen and police women, and then there are police officers of rank. Those higher-ranking officers make crucial decisions and grant authority to average officers to act.

It's exactly the same in the Spirit realm. We may have the presence of the power of the Holy Ghost in us, but unless God, who is the Chief Administrator, speaks or commands, we are to stand and wait for His direction to act.

Whatever we do, we must be "on the same page" with God. This is the basis for any healing ministry:

Then he called his twelve disciples together, and gave them power and authority over all devils, and to cure diseases. And he sent them to preach the kingdom of God, and to heal the sick. Luke 9:1-2

> *We must ask for God's mercy, and we must seek Him with the humility and faith of a child!*

In the event that we do not know God's divine and perfect will for a particular case, we can only ask for His mercy. That's what happened in the case of Epaphroditus.

The Lord is glorified when the sick are healed, and all men give Him praise, so the healing ministry is an important one. The apostles never failed in this ministry, and we, too, can avoid failure. This, however, requires that we wait for both the power and the authority to act.

This, then, is our only other option as we consider God's will for us and seek healing. We must ask for His mercy, and we must seek Him with the humility and faith of a child. This is an Epaphroditus deliverance, for, as we have seen, God had mercy on him:

> *For indeed he was sick nigh unto death: but God had mercy on him; and not on him only, but on me also, lest I should have sorrow upon sorrow.*
>
> Philippians 2:27

GOD'S MERCY DEMONSTRATED IN HEALING

Mercy, in regard to healing, is a demonstration of the compassion of God to men, delivering them without the assistance of any human instrument.

The words of Philippians 2:27 are the words of Paul, the apostle, who could have prayed for Epaphroditus' deliverance, but, as previously noted, apparently he did not. Therefore we can only conclude that Paul, who was filled with the Holy Spirit, did not receive the necessary authority from Christ to pray for his sick friend. If he had done so without God's express authority, it would have been presumptuous, and God cannot bless disobedience. Paul, who on one occasion, obeyed God and was able to save two hundred and seventy-six souls from death and give them the opportunity for salvation (see Acts 27:37-44), knew that without God he could do nothing.

Continuous Healings?

When the Lord has healed us once, we then look for that same miracle time and time again. This was Wendy's experience, after she received the touch of God that first time. She remained cancer-free for three years, but then it returned, and this time she was not healed. This presents a question for many. How many times will the Lord heal us in a lifetime?

Will our Lord stop healing us when we're seventy-eight? Eighty-eight? Ninety-eight? One hundred and eight? The answer is that we don't know, but there has to come a moment when He no longer heals us. If not, we would live on forever. Healing miracles are always subject to the sovereignty and will of God. He alone controls man's destiny.

King Hezekiah was told that the healing he received was for a limited time (fifteen years), so when he came to the appointed time for his departure, he knew that it was no longer possible to look for additional healing. God's ways are *"past finding out"*:

> *For God hath concluded them all in unbelief, that he might have mercy upon all. O the depth of the riches both of the wisdom and knowledge of God! how unsearchable are his judgments, and his ways past finding out!*   Romans 11:32-33

THE SICK ARE NOT FORSAKEN

To be sick is not a sin, and the sick are not forsaken by God. The work of ministry was always on Wendy's heart, despite the affliction she suffered. In times like these, afflicted saints can still minister to others, just as if they were healthy. Jesus loves us just the same (sick or well), and we all have the promise of His presence, giving us strength to tell the world that He lives.

In fact, the opportunity for ministering to others is strengthened in such times. Through the sickness we suffer, we actually become more like Jesus than we are when in good health, and the desire to give to and seek good for others is never greater. Our thoughts are now more focused on the God who can do all things.

Lazarus, Jesus' close friend, got sick and his sister sent an urgent message to Jesus:

Lord, behold, he whom thou lovest is sick. John 11:3

Lazarus' sickness didn't change his love for Jesus, and it certainly didn't change Jesus' love for him. Jesus' love for us never changes, and our love for Him shouldn't change either—whether we are sick or well.

Wendy had two more years of life left here, even though they would be years filled with *"light affliction"* (2 Corinthians 4:17). As Paul told the Romans, the wisdom and ways of God are often at work in our lives, even though we are unable to see its depth and beauty.

What is important to ailing saints is that they have

truth. Truth delivers us from fear and empty hope. Only God delegates the power and the authority for healing.

THE DISCIPLES OF JESUS
AND THE HEALING MINISTRY

Jesus sent the disciples out to minister, and He gave them authority to heal and to set captives free. Still, He refused to answer those men who questioned Him as to who had given Him this authority or by what authority He acted.

He had the same power and authority at that moment as He had after He had suffered death and Hell and then been resurrected. He is, the writer of Hebrews declares, *"the same yesterday, and to-day, and for ever"* (Hebrews 13:8). It was our Lord who gave healing power and authority to Moses, so that those who looked upon the brazen serpent were healed from their poisonous bites (see Numbers 21:8-9).

And what was Jesus' answer to the religious leaders of His day? It was given in the moment He empowered His own and sent them forth. *"They departed, and went through the towns, preaching the gospel, and healing every where"*:

> *And he said unto them, Take nothing for your jour-*
> *ney, neither staves, nor scrip, neither bread, neither*
> *money; neither have two coats apiece. And whatso-*
> *ever house ye enter into, there abide, and thence de-*
> *part. And whosoever will not receive you, when ye go*

out of that city, shake off the very dust from your feet for a testimony against them. And they departed, and went through the towns, preaching the gospel, and healing every where. Luke 9:3-6

We know now that without the authority given by God no one can expect to see deliverance from sickness. It is true that Jesus never failed in His deliverance, and the apostles (after the day of Pentecost) never failed in their deliverance, but this was because they were always "on the same page" with the Father, and the will of God was perfected through their lives of constant obedience. They understood what it meant to speak under the authority of God, guided by the power of the Holy Ghost, and we can do that too—when we get "on the same page" with Jehovah.

It has always been true:

> *Jesus sent the disciples out to minister, and He gave them authority to heal and to set captives free!*

God also bearing them witness, both with signs and wonders, and with divers miracles, and gifts of the Holy Ghost, according to his own will. Hebrews 2:4

Absolutely nothing happens apart from the will of God Almighty!

It's All About God

We can easily see, from the standpoint of God's Word, that healing is all about God, and that we are nothing more than instruments in His hand. Therefore, it is necessary that we are obedient and learn to work in submission to His authority.

It is God's divine and sovereign choice who will speak for Him and the words He will place in their hearts and minds through the operation of the Holy Spirit, so that all the glory and praise will be unto Him and Him alone. Without exception, no one will ever share His glory, for our God is a *"jealous God"* (Exodus 20:5).

Therefore, we (mere messengers that we are) must never be worshipped. God would never share His glory with a messenger. Balaam had to learn this lesson the hard way. Like many today, he became a prophet for profit. But God overruled Balaam's mind, and made him speak what *He* had ordained, not what the for-profit prophet had in his own heart.

When the devil came to tempt Jesus in the wilderness, He said to him, *"Get thee behind me, Satan: for it is written, Thou shalt worship the Lord thy God, and him only shalt thou serve"* (Luke 4:18). Even Jesus refused to take the glory reserved for the Father.

So when God is ready to minister healing to the sick, we need, in order of importance, first, the divine power, then, the divine authority, next, the divinely selected words, and finally, the complete obedience of the chosen vessel. That's a sure recipe for a miracle.

THE TESTIMONY OF A KING

Hezekiah didn't go to a physician, but if he had, he might have been told that he had very little time left here on this earth. He might have been diagnosed with some form of cancer, and he might have been given a time frame for survival. But those are only guesses on any doctor's part. Our times are in God's hands, and He chose to give Hezekiah fifteen more years.

First, though, God, in His sovereign will, sent His prophet to speak exactly what the Holy Spirit had placed on his mind, and he was faithful to speak it:

In those days was Hezekiah sick unto death. And the prophet Isaiah the son of Amoz came to him, and said unto him, Thus saith the LORD, Set thine house in order; for thou shalt die, and not live.   2 Kings 20:1

It was then that Hezekiah did some serious praying, and God sent the prophet back with another message:

And it came to pass, afore Isaiah was gone out into the middle court, that the word of the LORD came to him, saying, Turn again, and tell Hezekiah the captain of my people, Thus saith the LORD, the God of David thy father, I have heard thy prayer, I have seen thy tears: behold, I will heal thee: on the third day thou shalt go up unto the house of the LORD. And I will add unto thy days fifteen years. 2 Kings 20:4-6

Only God can determine when a man or woman's time has come.

> *Only God can determine when a man or woman's time has come!*

USE CAUTION WHEN PRAYING FOR THE SICK

It can sometimes be a disaster to ask people to pray for the sick, whether it's in a private home, or in a hospital or church. Wherever it occurs, I have a word of caution. If you are trying to speak for God, then you'd better hear from Heaven first.

It's never very acceptable to tell other Christians how they should pray or what they should say in prayer, but too many times, people say the most unacceptable things. They even preach through their prayer, as if their words were coming directly from the throne room of Heaven. In the process, many promises are made to the sick, assurances that often turn out to be misguided. This is very sad!

Unless you are authorized to do so, it is rebellion against God to tell a sick person that God is going to heal them or that the Lord is saying to them, at that moment, that they will rise from their sickness. We must learn to pray with understanding. And it's downright ignorant to pray for the impossible without the power and authority of God to back it up.

All saints should read how Paul responded to the administration of the Holy Spirit in dealing with sickness. He left everything up to God, as he sought His mercy. The Holy Spirit will tell you what to say and when to say it. Wait for the time and place and the God-given words of deliverance.

Most of any prayer should be composed of thanksgiving and praise to God for what He has already done for us. For the rest, we must wait for understanding.

I KNOW WHAT IT IS TO BE HEALED

In December of 1993, I received a great healing of my own. I was returning to New York City from a visit to my native Trinidad. There I had preached at a local church one Sunday morning a message entitled "The Gospel According to Jesus." After preaching that day, I began passing blood. I couldn't eat for several days and became very weak. I was sure that I was dying.

The night before my departure to New York the devil tried everything to kill me. I was taken to the very brink of death. There was no one with me to lay hands on me and pray, but God, in His mercy, helped me through the night. I kept thinking that I just needed to get back to New York so that I could get the necessary medical attention. As it turned out, God just wanted me to get in the air.

At thirty-two thousand feet in the air, Jesus healed me, and by the time I arrived at John F. Kennedy International Airport, my energy had been restored. Only six hours before, I had been a dying man, unable to carry an attaché case, but now I had enough energy to lift all of my suitcases. The bleeding had stopped, and I was free and perfectly healed by the mercy and grace of a loving and caring Jesus.

At the time, I didn't really understand what a miracle it was. Sometime during the following weeks, I decided to go on a fast, and during that fast, I didn't use a certain medication I had been on for a while. When the fast was ended, I was convicted by the Holy Spirit to stop using it altogether. I obeyed, and I have been well ever since.

Alleluia! What a Savior!

But is every saint to be healed of every sickness? Surely not. And only God knows His perfect will in this regard.

Are we alone in all of this? Never! *Never Alone!* ✻

CHAPTER 7

SICKNESS, NO RESPECTER OF PERSONS

For he longed after you all, and was full of heaviness, because that ye had heard that he had been sick. For indeed he was sick nigh unto death: but God had mercy on him; and not on him only, but on me also, lest I should have sorrow upon sorrow.

Philippians 2:26-27

Affliction is humbling to those who suffer it, and it should move to compassion all those who are aware of what others are suffering. In this passage, the Lord shows us the compassion and empathy of the great apostle Paul as he identified with his brother Epaphroditus in his trial of faith. Paul desperately wanted his partner in ministry to live and not die, and yet it seems apparent that he did not directly pray for his healing. Why? As I have noted previously, to me the answer is simple: he had not received authority from God to do it.

No Respecter of Persons

> *Believers are called upon to bear one another's burdens, demonstrating this same compassion!*

Sickness is no respecter of persons, and I can empathize with what Paul experienced. As Wendy got progressively worse, I rejected every prognosis offered by her doctors and nurses. They were quick to present me with the medical and scientific predictions for my beloved partner of so many years, but I didn't want to embrace their vision of the future for her life. I disagreed with what they said would happen, and still she was taken from me.

Sickness comes to us all, and it comes in one of several ways:

1. Some sickness is hereditary in nature.
2. Some sickness comes about through careless and reckless living because of ignorance and rebellion.
3. Some sickness is communicable (we catch it from others).
4. Some sickness is a result of natural causes (like wear

and tear on our bodies and their natural breakdown as we age).

5. And some sickness is definitely the work of Satan (see Luke 13:16).

Paul was humbled and concerned about the future of his ministry companion. He was humbled, most of all, that there was nothing he could do to relieve his friend of his suffering. Believers are called upon to bear one another's burdens, demonstrating this same compassion, as we witness the afflictions of our brothers and sisters in Christ, going through their times of testing. If this compassion goes deep enough, it will cause us to give up the things we have valued as most important in our lives. When a loved one is suffering, going out to buy the latest model of something is our last priority. Instead, we choose to suffer with them.

THE INESCAPABLE REALITY

The inescapable reality is that affliction comes to the educated, as well as to the unlearned; to the wealthy, as well as to the poor; to the king, the president and the governor, as well as to the lowliest member of society. It comes to the homeowner, as well as the tenant; to doctors and nurses, as well as to their patients; to correctional officers, as well as to their charges; to pastors, as well as to their congregations; to the righteous, as well as to the ungodly. There is no fortress here on earth that we could enter to hide from this unwelcome intruder.

85

NEVER ALONE!

Sickness is a constant reminder to us that we should number our days and begin to work toward doing what our God has said we came here to do. For His part, Jesus said that He had come here to do His Father's will and to finish His work. What is your mission on earth?

Don't Be Ashamed

Sickness is nothing to be ashamed of. Just because you're sick doesn't mean that you have sinned or failed God. The only thing that should cause us shame is failure or disobedience to the will of God and His Word. Feelings of shame over sickness are fleshly. We all want to look our best and be our best, and when we can't, it bothers us.

It's nice to feel good and look good, but if it's not possible, then we haven't failed. And if we feel sick, we need to face that fact squarely. Denying it doesn't help anyone. We know that Jesus understands, and if He understands, then it doesn't matter what others may think or say.

Peter wrote:

If ye be reproached for the name of Christ, happy are ye ; for the spirit of glory and of God resteth upon you; on their part he is evil spoken of, but on your part he is glorified. But let none of you suffer as a murderer, or as a thief, or as an evildoer, or as a busybody in other men's matters. Yet if any man suffer as a Christian, let him not be ashamed; but let him glorify God on this behalf. 1 Peter 4:14-16

86

The Spirit of God helps to overcome a sense of guilt and shame by comforting us with the promises of the Word of God. It is also important to remember, in these moments, our testimonies from the past and those of other believers. We overcome *"by the blood of the Lamb, and by the word of [our] testimony"* (Revelation 12:11). Rehearsing past testimonies will deliver us during attacks against our emotions.

EVEN PROPHETS GET SICK AND STILL MINISTER

The prophet Elisha became sick, and yet his zeal for God never diminished. The mind of Christ in us never gets old and wrinkled, just these mortal bodies. When Jesus was suffering on the cross, He was bearing the most agonizing sufferings ever known to man, and yet He was functioning mentally, understanding everything that was going on around Him.

Elisha fulfilled his last duty as a man of God, still speaking as a prophet, not a sick man trying to cling to the threads of life. His passion and determination never wavered, even in his final moments, when his strength was failing. He was still able to show his anger at the lack of zeal demonstrated by the actions (or inactions) of King Joash:

Now Elisha was fallen sick of his sickness whereof he died. And Joash the king of Israel came down unto him, and wept over his face, and said, O my father,

87

my father, the chariot of Israel, and the horsemen thereof.

And Elisha said unto him, Take bow and arrows. And he took unto him bow and arrows.

And he said to the king of Israel, Put thine hand upon the bow. And he put his hand upon it: and Elisha put his hands upon the king's hands.

And he said, Open the window eastward. And he opened it.

Then Elisha said, Shoot. And he shot. And he said, The arrow of the LORD's deliverance, and the arrow of deliverance from Syria: for thou shalt smite the Syrians in Aphek, till thou have consumed them.

And he said, Take the arrows. And he took them.

And he said unto the king of Israel, Smite upon the ground. And he smote thrice, and stayed. And the man of God was wroth with him, and said, Thou shouldest have smitten five or six times; then hadst thou smitten Syria till thou hadst consumed it: whereas now thou shalt smite Syria but thrice. 2 Kings 13:14-19

The man of God was so zealous to finish the ministry he had received from the Lord that he showed more interest in it and the welfare of the nation of Israel than he did in his own physical well-being. How amazing!

How could that be? All I can say is that Elisha's faith in the promise of eternal life remained steadfast. Perhaps he was remembering how he had seen his predecessor, Elijah, being taken up to Heaven. Just as Elijah finished his final mission before he left this world, so too Elisha would find his place in that eternal paradise if he was able to finish his course with joy.

GOD IS NOT ANGRY WITH YOU

As we previously noted, when the sisters of Lazarus saw how sick their brother was, they sent for Jesus to come and heal him:

> *Therefore his sisters sent unto him, saying, Lord, behold, he whom thou lovest is sick.*
>
> John 11:3

Elisha's faith in the promise of eternal life remained steadfast!

Lazarus was Jesus' friend, and He has also called us friends. Jesus loves us too, and He died for us, revealing Himself as *"a friend that sticketh closer than a brother"* (Proverbs 18:24). He is not angry with us. He prayed that the love the Father had for Him might be deposited in us. His love for us is without reservation, and it's totally unconditional. Our only qualification for His Love is accepting His atonement through His blood.

RESIST ALL FEAR

So what should we do when we suffer illness? For one, resist all fear.

What is fear? It is expecting evil to visit you in the future. If, instead, we look for God's promises, we can overcome fear.

The mind is fertile ground where the enemy can often plant his negative thoughts, but when our faith is expecting something good to visit us, expecting God to do something good for us in every situation, this puts the mind in a receiving mode. Nothing can beat positive expectations of what tomorrow will be like.

Worrying is a sign that we are not expecting good, but rather have a fear that something will go wrong. Resist the devil at the moment such thoughts go through your mind. Rebuke his thoughts and their attack on your mind. Then rejoice that you are delivered to serve the Lord without fear all the days of your life:

That he would grant unto us, that we being delivered out of the hand of our enemies might serve him without fear, in holiness and righteousness before him, all the days of our life. Luke 1:74-75

RESIST THE SPIRIT OF ANGER

What often happens, as we have noted, is that when we suffer sickness or one of our loved ones suffers sickness, we get angry with God. But did Job get angry? Oh, he may have been angry with the physicians of his day, for they promised and then they couldn't deliver. (Sadly, as also noted, there are also faith healers who promise what only God can deliver.) Job, in his anger, called those who were ministering to him *"physicians of no value"*:

> *What ye know, the same do I know also: I am not inferior unto you. Surely I would speak to the Almighty, and I desire to reason with God. But ye are forgers of lies, ye are all physicians of no value. O that ye would altogether hold your peace! and it should be to your wisdom.*   Job 13:2-5

Job was telling them, in no uncertain terms, that they were good for nothing. They could not help him, and so they were of no use to him right then.

He also called on these men to stop speaking. *"Hold your peace,"* he said. They were offering so many conflicting ideas, and their constant talking was like so much babble. What he needed was for them to shut up and give him some peace.

In his anger, Job told these men that he seemed to know about as much as they did, so it was not really possible for them to help him. The best thing they could do was just be quiet. Sometimes silence is the best thing you can offer the sick. If you have nothing constructive to contribute, let the sick rest in peace.

RESIST THE DEVIL

We are commanded in the Scriptures not to *"give place to the devil"* (Ephesians 4:27). When he attacks our minds, we must find something positive to speak against that thought. We can destroy evil thoughts by speaking the Word of God.

Once we have given place to the devil, we are left with the enormous task of getting him out. That causes us to use and lose spiritual energy, as we battle this unwanted houseguest. He comes in quite easily, but it's always a battle to get him out.

> *We are not destined to fall under the weight of these trials!*

Anger is something we all experience in times of sickness, whether we recover from the affliction or not. But such a period of affliction, in every case, is just temporary. The afflicted saint is delivered one way or another.

During periods of illness, therefore, we must never allow the enemy to keep us in bondage to any negative spirits. We can escape this fate by *"pray[ing] always,"* as Jesus commanded:

Watch ye therefore, and pray always, that ye may be accounted worthy to escape all these things that shall come to pass, and to stand before the Son of man. Luke 21:36

TO BE CONSECRATED TO GOD IS TO BE FOREARMED AGAINST ALL AFFLICTION

Jesus has given the members of the Body of Christ a warning concerning our sufferings and tribulations in this life. We are not destined to fall under the weight of these trials. Instead, they come to make us strong. The Gospel singer, Andrea Crouch, wrote a line that says, *"These trials only come to make us strong."*

The unredeemed, without hope, will always fall under the weight of their sufferings, and they have no hope beyond this life. The child of God cannot afford to allow these *"light afflictions"* to control or derail his faith in Jehovah God. Sanctification builds our spiritual immune system and prepares us for the unexpected.

Sickness will come to us all. What is important is how we will handle it when it comes. And when you're sick, are you alone? Never! *Never Alone!*　　　　　　✳

PART II

WHAT
WENDY ROBERTS
TAUGHT US

CHAPTER 8

SHE WAS A MODERNDAY HANNAH

And she was in bitterness of soul, and prayed unto the
LORD, and wept sore. And she vowed a vow.

1 Samuel 1:10-11

Wendy Roberts was a modernday Hannah.

God hears the prayers of consecrated saints, those
whose hearts are toward Him and for His glory. Hannah
came to the realization that if she gave glory to God in
her heart there was no reason that He, in His mercy and
tenderness, would deny her the thing she was asking of
Him. How many years did she wait for the blessings of
God to be her portion? It's anyone's guess, but it's probably safe to say that she had waited for many years

already. Now she decided that she could wait no longer, and so she poured out her heart to the Lord. In this time of divine desperation, God answered her cry.

Praying and Vowing

Notice that Hannah prayed and vowed at the same time. Let us add a few more verses of the context:

And she was in bitterness of soul, and prayed unto the Lord, and wept sore. And she vowed a vow, and said, O Lord of hosts, if thou wilt indeed look on the affliction of thine handmaid, and remember me, and not forget thine handmaid, but wilt give unto thine handmaid a man child, then I will give him unto the Lord all the days of his life, and there shall no razor come upon his head. And it came to pass, as she continued praying before the Lord, that Eli marked her mouth.

1 Samuel 1:10-12

The Lord is perfect, and when the hearts of the righteous call out to Him, He will always hear. How He responds depends on His divine will. He hears the cries of a broken and contrite spirit, and He must, for He has promised it in His Word.

In this case, Hannah's lips moved, but no sound was heard. God doesn't require loud prayers; He can hear even our whispered petitions. Hannah prayed earnestly, knowing that God heard the song of the soul:

Now Hannah, she spake in her heart; only her lips moved, but her voice was not heard: therefore Eli thought she had been drunken. And Eli said unto her, How long wilt thou be drunken? put away thy wine from thee.

And Hannah answered and said, No, my lord, I am a woman of a sorrowful spirit: I have drunk neither wine nor strong drink, but have poured out my soul before the LORD. Count not thine handmaid for a daughter of Belial: for out of the abundance of my complaint and grief have I spoken hitherto.

Then Eli answered and said, Go in peace: and the God of Israel grant thee thy petition that thou hast asked of Him.

1 Samuel 1:13-17

> *The Holy Spirit is the power that works for the performing of miracles in the womb!*

The Holy Spirit is the power that works for the performing of miracles in the womb, and the moment the God of Israel authorized the healing in Hannah's heart from her grief, the next move of the Spirit was to perform the miracle of restoration in her womb, so that she could receive seed for conception.

It's so comforting to know that the Lord remembers

our need. From that day forward, Hannah was no longer sad. She knew that God had answered her prayer:

*And she said, Let thine handmaid find grace in thy sight. So the woman went her way, and did eat, and her countenance was no more sad. And they rose up in the morning early, and worshipped before the L*ORD*, and returned, and came to their house to Ramah.*

1 Samuel 1:18-19

We meditate on what we hear, and if we hear nothing good, we meditate on negative things. If we hear a good word, then we have a seed planted in our minds that will eventually cause a tree to sprout and spiritual fruit to be borne. The immediate manifestation of it will be joy and a persevering spirit that will block out any spirit of depression and defeat. Hannah now had the word of comfort to meditate on, and this was manifested in her expression of joy. She was no longer sad.

Every believer must remember the words of the Scriptures and keep them in their heart. This is the manner in which we guard our hearts. Hannah was now waiting for the blessing, the miracle. She was trusting the word she had received from Eli, and she was trusting the mercy of a faithful God. And it worked:

*And Elkanah knew Hannah his wife; and the L*ORD *remembered her. Wherefore it came to pass, when the time was come about after Hannah had conceived, that*

*she bare a son, and called his name Samuel, saying,
Because I have asked him of the LORD.*

1 Samuel 1:19-20

WENDY DID THE SAME

Wendy, too, knew what it was to be barren and to pray for a child. In fact, she did this for nearly ten years, weeping and praying before the Lord from 1976 to 1985, until her answer came. As with Hannah, God remembered Wendy. He will always remember the prayer of those who pray, weep and vow in the earnestness of their hearts.

But believing God for a child is much more than weeping. Thanksgiving is also an integral part of the prayer life of a consecrated woman. Just look at the heartfelt praise and thanksgiving that burst forth from the heart of Hannah. She was not ashamed to confess that God was her only hope.

This is important, for the Bible declares that promotion does not come from the east or from the west, but only from God Himself, and that He alone is the Judge. He puts down one, and He raises up another (see Psalm 75:6-7). In His hand is the divine scepter that dictates promotion and blessing, all according to His will.

After the manifestation, or the demonstration, of God's miraculous power in our lives, we cannot hold back the joy that builds up in our soul, and there comes forth from the spirit of praise and thanksgiving that the Holy Spirit brings to our hearts. The pattern is always the same. First we pray and seek the face of God, waiting for His perfect time to manifest our desire. Then we receive the blessings, and when the manifestation of God's faithfulness has become a reality, we join together in praising Him.

Here, then, is the praise and thanksgiving of a consecrated woman of God:

> *Thanks be to God, for He is One who, when He promises, never fails!*

There is none holy as the LORD: for there is none beside thee: neither is there any rock like our God. Talk no more so exceeding proudly; let not arrogancy come out of your mouth: for the LORD is a God of knowledge, and by him actions are weighed. The bows of the mighty men are broken, and they that stumbled are girded with strength.

1 Samuel 2:2-4

After the answer has come from the throne of God, the believer is overwhelmed with the spirit of praise and thanksgiving, and will exalt God in gratitude, giving praise to the One who hears and answers prayer:

They that were full have hired out themselves for bread; and they that were hungry ceased: so that the barren hath born seven; and she that hath many children is *waxed feeble. The L*ord *killeth, and maketh alive: he bringeth down to the grave, and bringeth up [this is prophetic, pointing to the coming of the resurrected Lord]. The L*ord *maketh poor, and maketh rich: he bringeth low, and lifteth up. He raiseth up the poor out of the dust, and lifteth up the beggar from the dunghill, to set them among princes.*   1 Samuel 2:5-8

Wendy prayed the prayer of Hannah, but she received the blessing of Sarah, the wife of Abraham. Hannah's prayer brought her Samuel and then three more sons and two daughters. Sarah received just one son, and she called his name Isaac. Wendy did the same (Isaac is our son's middle name). These are the miracles our Lord does.

Our God Never Fails

Thanks be to God, for He is One who, when He promises, never fails. For this reason, any praying, consecrated woman of God can make their petition to the Lord, and the same Lord who answered women of old will answer—as long as the expressed need is not to be consumed upon a lustful desire. Just as long as our prayers are balanced, subjectively and objectively, God will be merciful to us.

But All Blessings Come with Responsibility

All blessings come with responsibility. When Samuel came, this was evident. He bore an awesome responsibility, and so does every child who is miraculously born. Thank God that we were able to bring our son up in the ways of the Lord, so we have the assurance that when he is old, he will not depart from them.

Yes, Wendy was a modernday Hannah, and you can be too.

Do you have to stand alone in all of this? Never! *Never Alone!*   ✻

CHAPTER 9

SHE WAS A WOMAN OF PRAYER

And it came to pass in those days, that he went out into a mountain to pray, and continued all night in prayer to God. And when it was day, he called unto him his disciples: and of them he chose twelve, whom also he named apostles. Luke 6:12-13

Wendy Roberts was a woman of prayer.

There cannot be victory in the life of the believer until prayer becomes a disciplined factor in our lives. We cannot approach this function as a ritual but must see it as a necessary and most important part of our everyday lives. We face an enemy, and we must do it with weapons that are not carnal, but spiritual, and *"mighty*

105

through God to the pulling down of strong holds" (2 Corinthians 10:4).

> *It was impossible even for Jesus to fulfill His ministry of great sacrifice without the anointing that comes through prayer and fasting!*

As we approach this fellowship with God, we are also telling Him, from the sincerity of our hearts, how much we love Him and delight in the ministry of prayer. This was a ministry that Jesus fully embraced.

THE IMPORTANCE OF FASTING AND PRAYER

In preparation for His ministry, Jesus fasted forty days and forty nights. It was impossible even for Him to fulfill His ministry of great sacrifice without the anointing that comes through prayer and fasting. Therefore, the preparation for any task of spiritual dimensions should be preceded by a reasonable period of prayer and fasting.

Moses, too, was in the presence of Jehovah for forty days and forty nights. He was the chosen leader to fulfill the promise of God to the children of Israel. God's promise to Abraham had been to deliver His chosen from Egypt after four hundred years of slavery in that land, and Moses was the man to do the job. He could not do it alone, however, so he sought God in fasting and prayer.

Prayer became a lifestyle for Jesus. He didn't just pray once; He made prayer a habit. He was God in the flesh, and yet He did not do anything without first spending time with His heavenly Father.

Jesus prayed all night before choosing His disciples the next day. This shows us that we must pray as long as necessary to prepare for whatever task is at hand. He also made a habit of rising early in the morning to seek the Father:

> *And in the morning, rising up a great while before day, he went out, and departed into a solitary place, and there prayed.*   Mark 1:35

The fact that even Jesus rose early in the morning teaches those of us who are filled with the Holy Spirit not to just take life easy. We should be willing to sacrifice some sleep to meet God early each day. After all, we are nothing without Him.

PREPARING FOR THE CHALLENGE OF THE DAY

Notice, in the case of Jesus, that as soon as the day had begun, there was a challenging task awaiting Him, a leper who needed deliverance. Often we may not know exactly what specific task will await us, so it's important that we're always ready and well prepared through the power of the Spirit to overcome whatever we might be called upon to face.

The leper approached Jesus:

And there came a leper to him, beseeching him, and kneeling down to him, and saying unto him, If thou wilt, thou canst make me clean. And Jesus, moved with compassion, put forth his hand, and touched him, and saith unto him, I will; be thou clean. And as soon as he had spoken, immediately the leprosy departed from him, and he was cleansed. Mark 1:40-42

Jesus was ready for this, and the work was accomplished. In the same way, through prayer, he was ready every day. When the need arose to feed thousands of people, He calmly took a few loaves of bread and a few fish and met their need. On many occasions, He healed all that were sick.

THE COMBINATION OF HOLINESS, PRAYER AND FASTING

There were three important elements to Wendy's life of prayer and we find these same three elements in the kind of prayer life that has brought miracles for as long as men and women have been lifting up their voices to seek the Lord's help.

All three elements are essential. Prayer alone is not enough. God also requires that the prayer be uttered in holiness of heart, and the prayer must sometimes be combined with fasting. Wendy was a woman of fasting, but when she became ill, I was led to dedicate myself to many days of fasting for her deliverance and for the anointing of the Holy Spirit in her life.

Every sanctified husband is responsible and account-able to God to remain in that *"secret place of the most High"* in humility (Psalm 91:1). What is that *"secret place"* the psalmist David spoke about? It's a place of holiness and prayer. We can actually hide in the holiness of Almighty God, and we do it through the righteousness of the Lord Jesus Christ.

PRAYING IN THE SPIRIT

The New Testament weapon of prayer, available to men and women alike, adds additional force. That weapon is praying in the Spirit, and Paul has declared that the Holy Spirit helps us in our weaknesses:

> *Likewise the Spirit also helpeth our infirmities: for we know not what we should pray for as we ought: but the Spirit itself maketh intercession for us with groanings which cannot be uttered. And he that searcheth the hearts knoweth what is the mind of the Spirit, because he maketh intercession for the saints according to the will of God.*   Romans 8:26-27

So the Spirit also makes intercession for us *"according to the will of God."* What better way could there be to pray? When we pray in the Spirit, it is as if Jesus Himself is praying to the Father, and we know that when Jesus prayed to the Father (during His time here on earth), the Father always answered, because Jesus and the Father are one.

We, today, have the same responsibility that Jesus left to His disciples when they had failed in their efforts to deliver a man who came to them for help. Jesus had not yet sacrificed His life on Calvary, yet He gave the disciples a strong and challenging commitment—fasting and prayer as the key to the impossible:

> *And he said unto them, This kind can come forth by nothing, but by prayer and fasting.*   Mark 9:29

The men and women of the New Testament did not stop fasting and praying after the Holy Spirit was outpoured upon them. Even the apostle Paul fasted and prayed in situations where he desperately needed God's help, and he encouraged others to fast and pray:

> *And while the day was coming on, Paul besought them all to take meat, saying, This day is the fourteenth day that ye have tarried and continued fasting, having taken nothing.*   Acts 27:33

Their fasting and prayer paid off, as the ship was wrecked, but not one of them was hurt:

> *And falling into a place where two seas met, they ran the ship aground; and the forepart stuck fast, and re-*

mained unmovable, but the hinder part was broken with the violence of the waves.

They which could swim ... cast themselves first into the sea, and [got] to land. And the rest, some on boards, and some on broken pieces of the ship. And so it came to pass, that they escaped all safe to land.

Acts 27:41 and 43-44

In this case, fasting saved the lives of two hundred and seventy-six souls (see Acts 27:37). When we are consecrated saints of the Living God, we seek to do anything to save lost humanity. Fasting and prayer, directed by the Holy Ghost, is one of the most powerful weapons to accomplish this awesome task. Fasting works for them, releasing in us compassion for a sick and lost humanity, and in us, helping to deliver us from the spirit of pride.

Yes, Wendy Roberts was a woman of prayer, and you can be too.

Are we alone in all of this? Never! *Never Alone!* ✳

CHAPTER 10

SHE WAS THE ROCK OF OUR FAMILY

Every wise woman buildeth her house: but the foolish plucketh it down with her hands.   Proverbs 14:1

Wendy Roberts was the rock of our family, and the rock of every strong family is a woman who is blessed with two qualities: wisdom and holiness. These special graces that control her spirit are part of God's design for the consecrated woman.

Every man of God needs a wife with a resume that includes these qualities. She is the builder of her home, not a destroyer. She is a dedicated woman who rises up early to call upon God and is a faithful steward of the gifts with which He has endowed her. This all begins, of course, with the right kind of marriage.

Marriage Must Be Founded upon the Rock, Christ

A marriage founded upon the Rock, which is Christ, and the power of His guidance through the Holy Spirit, will always produce a lasting testimony and leave a legacy. Such testimonies tell the world that Christ is truly the answer, and such families are true representatives of Christ, the Bridegroom, and the Church, the Bride of Christ. It seems that saints like Wendy Roberts should be left to continue for many years on the earth because their lives have been such a powerful and strong testimony.

Strong women make strong marriages, and strong marriages make strong homes. The foundation of a home built upon the spiritual materials of honesty, love, truth, respectful communication, humility, financial discipline, sacrifice, compromise and temperance must prosper. Peace in any home is the work of the fruits of the Spirit, never the work of the flesh.

This particular saint was a consecrated woman of God with inner strength to give righteous counsel, as well as educational counsel, to students, and she did this faithfully in her capacity as a teacher—in spite of Department of Education restrictions.

A CONSECRATED WOMAN IS BLESSED
WITH PRACTICAL WISDOM

A consecrated woman is blessed with practical wisdom. She deals with facts and makes no decision based on emotions. With her, there is no impulse buying. Every transaction must be clearly investigated and evaluated before making a final decision. Financial stewardship is paramount because she believes that she is responsible for the blessings God sends our way.

No saint of God can afford to use the world's standard of living. We are commanded, rather, not to be conformed to this world, but to be transformed by the renewing of our minds and the adoption of the very mind of Christ (see Romans 12:2). Every man needs a woman with these qualities.

A consecrated woman is blessed with practical wisdom!

Who can find such a woman? Solomon asked that question too:

Who can find a virtuous woman? for her price is far above rubies. The heart of her husband doth safely trust in her, so that he shall have no need of spoil.
Proverbs 31:10-11

She's God's woman, and she always has a joyful smile

and words seasoned with salt, and they come forth from virtuous lips. The love of God that resides deep within her heart is expressed without reservation.

God can make every consecrated woman virtuous, with or without the help of her husband. However, with a man of God as her spiritual head, she can rise to her highest potential. A righteous helpmate makes the union more powerful. As the Scriptures note, one can chase a thousand, but two can *"put ten thousand to flight"* (Deuteronomy 32:30).

The Most Consecrated Woman in History

There is a lot that every woman alive today could learn from Mary, the most consecrated woman in history. She learned that when you cannot convince your husband, the Holy Ghost will do it.

Mary was given the unenviable task of telling Joseph, her espoused husband, that she was *"with child"* (Matthew 1:18). The Holy Ghost then took up the task that no woman on earth could effectively accomplish, dealing with his injured male ego. Most women today can't convince their husband on any given subject, even though they resort to the help of psychologists, psychiatrists and other professionals. Maybe it's time to trust the Lord completely.

Those of us who love the Lord know to seek the Holy Ghost for counsel. Why do we ask educated professionals to do what only a supernatural God can do? There is plenty that's too hard for professionals, but there is nothing too hard for our God.

MARY TRUSTED JESUS

Mary knew to take the peoples' problem to Jesus. When there was a serious problem and the people had no way of solving it, she went immediately to Him, to tell Him what was wrong. It is good when mothers can put their trust in their sons to solve problems that are too big for them:

> *And both Jesus was called, and his disciples, to the marriage. And when they wanted wine, the mother of Jesus saith unto him, They have no wine. Jesus saith unto her, Woman, what have I to do with thee? mine hour is not yet come. His mother saith unto the servants, Whatsoever he saith unto you, do it.*   John 2:2-5

If Mary trusted Jesus, her son, why can't we do the same today?

TRUE CONSECRATION RESULTS IN FINANCIAL DISCIPLINE

Another of the areas where we desperately need strong consecrated women today is in the realm of finances. Debt has swallowed us up in the twenty-first century, and debt will always bring us into bondage. In the Scriptures, we are called upon to *"owe no man any thing,"* we are told, *"The borrower is servant to the lender,"* we are warned of *"the deceitfulness of riches,"* and riches are called *"uncertain"*:

NEVER ALONE!

Owe no man any thing, but to love one another: for he that loveth another hath fulfilled the law.

Romans 13:8

The rich ruleth over the poor, and the borrower is servant to the lender.

Proverbs 22:7

And the cares of this world, and the deceitfulness of riches, and the lusts of other things entering in, choke the word, and it becometh unfruitful.

Mark 4:19

> **When are riches "uncertain"? They're always uncertain!**

Charge them that are rich in this world, that they be not highminded, nor trust in uncertain riches, but in the living God, who giveth us richly all things to enjoy.

1 Timothy 6:17

Indebtedness is a trap that impoverishes those who fall into it, but when the consecrated saint of God wisely remains debt free, he never has to worry about losing anything. Instead, he can enjoy *"godliness with contentment,"* which is *"great gain"* (1 Timothy 6:6).

Uncertain Riches

When are riches *"uncertain"*? They're always uncertain. Anything and everything on this earth is uncertain.

Whatever falls under the category of *things* can vanish in a moment's time.

Take for example the town of Plymouth on the beautiful island of Montserrat. This wonderful town, the capital of the small Caribbean nation, is situated on the seacoast, but today it is largely buried because it stood so near to what has become one of the world's most active volcanos.

In 1995, the Montserrat volcano began to show signs of imminent eruption. Ample warning was given, but still many could not believe that their beautiful town would be destroyed. When the mountain finally did explode, many lost their lives and fully two thirds of the area's inhabitants were forced to flee to other areas, as the once-thriving capital was left uninhabitable. Today the whole town lies covered with ash.

On one of our mission trips, I stood on the spot where that city once flourished. Under my feet were buried mansions with expensive European cars, all now entombed in solid ash.

The rest of that passage in 1 Timothy 6 says this:

That they do good, that they be rich in good works, ready to distribute, willing to communicate; laying up in store for themselves a good foundation against the time to come, that they may lay hold on eternal life.
1 Timothy 6:18-19

In all things, it is important to have the type of spirit and attitude to accept both the negative and the positive.

Whether things are going well or things are not going well, the believer should not *"stagger"* at the promises of God (Romans 4:20).

It is frightening to hear some saints say that they could not live poor and others insist that they don't know what they would do if they lost their wealth. There are even those who would actually commit suicide if their riches were lost and they had to go back to living a simple life in a small apartment somewhere.

Paul the apostle has some very important lessons for all of us:

> *But I rejoiced in the Lord greatly, that now at the last your care of me hath flourished again; wherein ye were also careful, but ye lacked opportunity. Not that I speak in respect of want: for I have learned, in whatsoever state I am, therewith to be content. I know both how to be abased, and I know how to abound: every where and in all things I am instructed both to be full and to be hungry, both to abound and to suffer need. I can do all things through Christ which strengtheneth me.*
>
> Philippians 4:10-13

We must remember that *"the kingdom of God is not meat and drink"* which money can buy. Rather, it is *"righteousness, and peace, and joy in the Holy Ghost"* (Romans 14:17). We have begun the life of enjoyment here as soon as we have been changed into the new nature and have become partakers of the divine nature of Jesus Christ our Lord. Money no longer rules us.

FOOD ADDICTION IS AN EVIL SPIRIT

One more area where a consecrated woman can make all the difference in a home is with food. Jesus said:

And take heed to yourselves, lest at any time your hearts be overcharged with surfeiting, and drunkenness, and cares of this life, and so that day come upon you unawares. Luke 21:34

In this passage Jesus spoke of a condition that is quite prevalent in our time, and it is hindering many Christians in the life of sanctification. It is *surfeiting*. Surfeiting, as we know it, is an excessive amount of eating and drinking, and it is not possible to speak of this topic without noting how very damning this sin is to the development of sanctification. We must not take this matter lightly.

Unfortunately, this kind of overindulgence has become a part of the popular culture in most western societies today and in other nations that copy this culture. Eating out is not the problem. That's fine. The problem is that no one seems to know when to stop.

The availability of fast food has led to faster eating, and faster eating has led to more overeating. The reality is that many of us are now addicted to food. An actual spirit has taken control of many, and it is an evil spirit, not of God.

NEVER ALONE!

Overeating has led to gluttony, and gluttony is certainly a sin. So we need help, and spiritual deliverance is the only way out. Wendy was wise in this regard.

Yes, Wendy was the rock of our family.

Were we now alone in all of this? Never! *Never Alone!*

✳

CHAPTER 11

SHE WAS NEVER LAZY

And the apostles gathered themselves together unto Jesus, and told him all things, both what they had done, and what they had taught. And He said unto them, Come ye yourselves apart into a desert place, and rest a while: for there were many coming and going, and they had no leisure so much as to eat. Mark 6:30-31

One of the most important elements of Wendy Roberts' blessing to our lives was her hard work and dedication to finishing everything she started and to finishing it well. Some people start many things, but finish nothing, and some do many things, but do nothing well. God, however, blesses a finished work and a work well done.

Jesus Set the Example

Jesus set the example for us on the cross of Calvary, when He said, *"It is finished"* (John 19:30). The Bible is filled with the records of faithful men and women who also finished the work God gave them to do.

Noah, for instance, finished the building of the ark:

> *Thus did Noah; according to all that God commanded him, so did he. And the LORD said unto Noah, Come thou and all thy house into the ark; for thee have I seen righteous before me in this generation.*
> Genesis 6:22-7:1

Jesus set the example for us on the cross of Calvary, when He said, "It is finished!"

In this beautiful passage, God shows that obedience is the secret to receiving the blessings of the finished work. And when God calls us *righteous* in this generation, we will surely experience the same blessings as Noah. How wonderful to be called *righteous* by the Righteous Judge of all the earth!

Moses finished his leadership role in bringing the people of Israel out of Egypt and through the wilderness and, along the way, the building of the wilderness Tabernacle. He also taught his people to work well:

> *According to all that the LORD commanded Moses, so the children of Israel made all the work. And Moses did look upon all the work, and, behold, they had done it as the LORD had commanded, even so had they done it: and Moses blessed them.* Exodus 39:42-43

There is a very important word found in these two passages. It describes the completion of the ark by Noah and the Tabernacle in the wilderness by Moses and the children of Israel. It is the word *all*. Both Noah and Moses did *all* that the Lord commanded them. They had the heart of the Lord through the Holy Spirit, and it imputed into their minds the specifications of needed constructions, and they built accordingly.

PAUL WAS ALSO DEDICATED TO HIS WORK

Paul was also a man dedicated to finishing his work:

> *For I am now ready to be offered, and the time of my departure is at hand. I have fought a good fight, I have finished my course, I have kept the faith: henceforth there is laid up for me a crown of righteousness, which the Lord, the righteous judge, shall give me at that day: and not to me only, but unto all them also that love his appearing.* 2 Timothy 4:6-8

Paul knew that he had finished his course, and that's an important thing to know. When this is the case, there will be no doubts in our minds when our Chief Commander calls us, his faithful soldiers, to our ultimate sabbatical.

THE APOSTLES FINISHED THEIR ASSIGNMENT

The apostles finished their assignment in the first century. It was to establish the Church in their generation, and they accomplished it through much affliction:

Confirming the souls of the disciples, and exhorting them to continue in the faith, and that we must through much tribulation enter into the kingdom of God.
Acts 14:22

The challenge for our generation is to know what our assignment is and, by the grace of God and the ministry of the anointing of the Holy Spirit, to finish it. We are all responsible and accountable to God to finish what we start, whether it be in the field of ministry or in the non-religious environment. God's standards remain the same for all.

WENDY'S ONE UNFINISHED WORK

For a time, Wendy kept an unfinished thesis for a masters degree in the closet. It would have to be submitted before the statute of limitations ran out, and in spite of all her other responsibilities, I encouraged her to finish the task. "Please don't give up at the finish line," I told her. "Your hard work over so many years and an investment of so much money should not be thrown away just because some professor said that education works against minorities. You are a majority with God on your side."

I could not accept that lie coming from the world of the prince of darkness. After all, God said that He didn't give us *"the spirit of fear; but of power, and of love, and of a sound mind"* (2 Timothy 1:7). God moved, and sent Wendy strength to overcome her weakness. As a result, the thesis was submitted on time, and the MA was successfully completed.

The reward of obedience came several years later, when she applied for a teaching position with the Department of Education. You can imagine that her MA came in very handy that day. Thank God that He had given her strength to finish the task.

CONSECRATED SAINTS ARE
DELIVERED FROM LAZINESS

Consecration delivers the believer from many of the emotional spirits that haunt him or her. A consecrated woman is not lazy, and she will follow the Lord Jesus and His example of a disciplined life in the work of ministry and of prayer. Jesus had to urge His disciples to come aside. They were very eager to continue the work. They had learned this from Jesus Himself:

NEVER ALONE!

*Jesus saith unto them, My meat is to do the will of him
that sent me, and to finish his work.*   John 4:34

Jesus demonstrated His determination to continue
working and finish all that He and the disciples had begun in ministering to the poor. They went so far as to
go beyond the time limit, even having no time for rest
or food, so that the day's task could be completed.

Before His life ended on the cross, Jesus was able to
finish all that the Father had sent Him to do:

*I have glorified thee on the earth: I have finished
the work which thou gavest me to do.*
                                              John 17:4

In His spirit, Christ accepted what He must do on
the cross and conditioned His soul for this final task.
Rather than think of Himself and what He would suffer, He concentrated on the glory that was to follow.

His death had been discussed much earlier, with
Moses and Elijah, on the Mount of Transfiguration:

*And, behold, there talked with him two men, which
were Moses and Elias: who appeared in glory, and
spake of his decease which he should accomplish at
Jerusalem.*   Luke 9:30-31

And still Jesus was willing to finish the task, whatever the cost.

JOHN THE BAPTIST FINISHED HIS WORK

John the Baptist finished his work in a very unusual manner. It was not a pleasant ending, but his work was fully accomplished. John had a radical message, for he knew well what his assignment was. And once he had put his hand to the plow, there was no turning back.

Some might have seen John's task as too humble, and yet it was profound. He was the fore-runner of Jesus. He prepared the way, and then he moved aside so that Jesus could be preeminent.

The truths that John preached caused him to have enemies and eventually, to be put to death at the hands of wicked men. He wasn't killed on the first attempt:

For John had said unto Herod, It is not lawful for thee to have thy brother's wife. Therefore Herodias had a quarrel against him, and would have killed him; but she could not.

Mark 6:18-19

In His spirit, Christ accepted what He must do on the cross and conditioned His soul for this final task!

129

NEVER ALONE!

But just because he failed once, the devil didn't give up. He is out to kill every single one of God's beloved servants. At the first opportunity, he continued to push his evil plan.

Our enemy is always looking for his opportunity to hurt us, but one thing we know: he cannot kill us before God's work is accomplished in us. Jesus finished His work, Paul finished his work and Moses finished his work. Would Jehovah God whom we serve allow us to fall into the hands of the enemy? We're His children.

The most important point in our lives here on earth will be the moment in which we enter into God's presence. For most of us, it will be a period of going through a shadow. Death is mysterious and therefore, inspires fear. But our Lord has promised to be with us. Every saint will eventually die, so we must not live in fear of that moment. When it comes, the angels of God will take good care of you.

Eventually, John's life had run its course:

And when the daughter of the said Herodias came in, and danced, and pleased Herod and them that sat with him, the king said unto the damsel, Ask of me whatsoever thou wilt, and I will give it thee. And he sware unto her, Whatsoever thou shalt ask of me, I will give it thee, unto the half of my kingdom. And she went forth, and said unto her mother, What shall I ask? And she said, The head of John the Baptist.

Mark 6:22-24

The verses that follow give a record of John's earthly end. The executioner was immediately called, and John was beheaded there in the prison. Then his head was brought in a charger and presented to the damsel as she had requested.

And when Wendy Roberts' life had run its course, I'm sure she heard the Master's words, "Well done, good and faithful servant." What will He say to you?

Are you alone as you face this challenge? Never! *Never Alone!* ✻

CHAPTER 12

SHE UNDERSTOOD THE BEAUTY OF HOLINESS

Whose adorning let it not be that outward adorning of plaiting the hair, and of wearing of gold, or of putting on of apparel; but let it be the hidden man of the heart, in that which is not corruptible, even the ornament of a meek and quiet spirit, which is in the sight of God of great price.   1 Peter 3:3-4

Wendy Roberts understood the beauty of holiness.

God's consecrated servants are seen through and through by the eyes of the Lord and must surrender their wills to Him. He knows us from the inside out, and despite what we profess to be on the outside, He already sees the real holiness (or lack of it) on the inside.

HOLINESS IS BEAUTIFUL

God designed holiness for beauty. Holiness is not uncleanness and indecency. God calls these *"an abomination."* The very place that God wants us to worship and pray and praise must have respect to the Holy Spirit. It must be clean, to represent Him and to have His people and His presence. God gave the best, and so He certainly deserves the best. When any man or woman says that they're presenting an offering to God and that offering appears to be filthy and indecent, don't be fooled by it. That person is just deceiving himself.

God said to Moses:

> *And thou shalt make holy garments for Aaron thy brother for glory and for beauty.*   Exodus 28:2

This beauty is a precious ornament that cannot be compared to gold or other elements of this world. Peter spoke of it as something so precious that it could not be corrupted. It could not be destroyed. Holiness has lasting potential.

The reflection of the holiness that dwells in us should be recognized on the outside, not only in the clothes we wear, but in our manner of expression as well. This includes our attitude, our speech and our conduct. Commands to cover all of these areas are clearly outlined in the Scripture, and we can't fool God:

> *The LORD is good, a strong hold in the day of trouble; and he knoweth them that trust in him.* Nahum 1:7

A consecrated man or woman knows the demands upon his or her life, the command from the Lord for us to be holy. He has given us a lifetime to spend on this earth, so we should have more than enough time to work on all the rough areas of our lives, so that when our time here is finished, we can present ourselves before God being holy.

In the case of Wendy, this became her daily exercise. She was continually seeking God's face to be sanctified by His Word.

SANCTIFICATION COMES THROUGH THE PRACTICAL APPLICATION OF THE WORD OF GOD

Sanctification is not to be attained by listening to good Gospel music or by listening to good Gospel preaching. These have their place, but holiness comes through the development of a Christ-centered life, one that has a practical and daily application of His Word.

Sanctification is not to be attained by listening to good Gospel music or by listening to good Gospel preaching!

The primary source of sanctification is the Word, and we all need more of it:

Follow peace with all men, and holiness, without which no man shall see the Lord. Hebrews 12:14

One day, we must all stand before the Judge of all the earth, and in that moment, we will not be able to blame anyone else for our lack. It is our personal responsibility to remain steadfast in our faith at all times.

In His very last command given before leaving the Earth, Jesus spoke of the times of the end and our accountability to Him through them:

And take heed to yourselves, lest at any time your hearts be overcharged with surfeiting, and drunkenness, and cares of this life, and so that day come upon you unawares. For as a snare shall it come on all them that dwell on the face of the whole earth. Watch ye therefore, and pray always, that ye may be accounted worthy to escape all these things that shall come to pass, and to stand before the Son of man.

Luke 21:34-36

ALL OF CREATION WILL STAND BEFORE HIM

The world seems to forget that one day all creation will stand before the Son of Man. You don't hear much of that in our present-day materialistic society, but it is real nevertheless. Thank God for the wisdom that gives His beloved saints more than enough time to know Him, even as Paul said:

That I may know him, and the power of his resurrection, and the fellowship of his sufferings, being made conformable unto his death.   Philippians 3:10

The last and most soul-searching desire of Paul was his desire to know Christ. He was not nearly as intrigued with the power to bring souls to Christ, heal the sick and demonstrate God's power in his ministry. He wanted to know Christ, the very Christ he would soon be standing before in the same way John the Baptist had wanted to know for sure that Jesus was the Promised One, or if he should wait for another.

We cannot be presumptuous about our righteousness. If we are, we may become self-righteous and hypocritical before God. Instead, we must seek to walk closer to God every day:

But I say unto you, That every idle word that men shall speak, they shall give account thereof in the day of judgment.   Matthew 12:36

This is Jesus Himself speaking to us about our need to become more conscious of our goal of holiness.

As we read the Word of God, we can hear the Holy Spirit speaking to us concerning our daily walk. It should lead us ever upward to the height of holiness:

Walk in wisdom toward them that are without, redeeming the time. Let your speech be alway with grace, seasoned with salt, that ye may know how ye ought to answer every man.   Colossians 4:5-6

NEVER ALONE!

This is another warning to guard our hearts in this perverse generation. What we see and hear have a great impact on our minds. And we now see unhealthy images every day in public places, and it's difficult for us to control that. It just comes as you go about your daily routine. At home, however, we *can* control much of the "junk" the media throws at us, by monitoring our radios and our television sets. There, in the sacredness of our homes, we are in control of what we listen to and what we look at.

We must feel the responsibility to guard our hearts. Peter warned those of his generation:

> *At home we can control much of the "junk" the media throws at us, by monitoring our radios and our television sets!*

Then Peter said unto them, Repent and be baptized every one of you in the name of Jesus Christ for the remission of sins, and ye shall receive the gift of the Holy Ghost. For the promise is unto you, and to your children, and to all that ... the Lord our God shall call. And with many other words did he testify and exhort, saying, Save yourselves from this untoward generation. Acts 2:38-40

Peter's warning was to escape from that *"untoward generation"* by being filled with the Holy Spirit. We need the same Spirit in us who was in Lot when he was *"vexed with the filthy conversation of the wicked"*:

> *And delivered just Lot, vexed with the filthy conversation of the wicked: (For that righteous man dwelling among them, in seeing and hearing, vexed his righteous soul from day to day with their unlawful deeds.)*
>
> 2 Peter 2:7-8

Each of us must feel that righteous indignation that builds in the heart and minds of a consecrated saint when he or she sees the depraved actions and expressions of this present world. Our generation is crooked and *"corrupt"*:

> *Let no corrupt communication proceed out of your mouth, but that which is good to the use of edifying, that it may minister grace unto the hearers. And grieve not the holy Spirit of God, whereby ye are sealed unto the day of redemption.* Ephesians 4:29-30

With us, there is another reason to remain unspotted. We represent the King of Kings and are ambassadors for our Lord, and this is not only true when we are in our Sunday religious mindset, with a Bible in our hands. We must also honor Him as the light to the world when we are in the company of unbelievers.

It always bothered Wendy that many who called

themselves saints of God dressed and behaved just like the ungodly. We should be the pace-setters for our families and our communities, and the world should learn from us—not the other way around.

Not a List of Do's and Don'ts

The holy life of the Christian is not about a list of do's and don'ts; it's about representing the King of Kings. The life that we live on earth right now should be an example of what Jesus would do if He were here in the flesh Himself. We must keep a constant vigil over our souls so that our actions may be accounted worthy unto eternal life:

> *For the Lord taketh pleasure in his people: he will beautify the meek with salvation.* Psalm 149:4

Wendy was ever conscious of this need and set a good example for us all.

Are we alone in all of this? Never! *Never Alone!*   ✳

CHAPTER 13

SHE UNDERSTOOD THE SOURCE OF TRUE HAPPINESS

Blessed and holy is he that hath part in the first resur-
rection: on such the second death hath no power, but
they shall be priests of God and of Christ, and shall
reign with him a thousand years.   Revelation 20:6

Wendy Roberts understood the source of true happiness.

When we realize that we are even now preparing for the thousand-year reign with Christ, there can be no greater joy. This is a process, an ongoing work of sanctification, and the believer has to do his part. Our humble part is simply obedience to the Word of God and submission to the convicting power and influence of the Holy Spirit.

As we prepare ourselves for the awesome responsibilities of the future, others are touched by our lives, directly and indirectly, and are challenged by our commitment to Christ

God is God, and so He provides all our needs, but He is also Lord, and so He rules over us!

WHAT IS HAPPINESS?

The word *happy* is recorded just twenty-eight times in the Bible, and yet achieving "happiness" is the desire of every human being. The problem is that many are deceived about the true definition of happiness and how it is achieved.

One of the important ingredients for happiness is security. To be safe and secure in life and free from fear is the hope of every saint of God. And happiness is the direct result of being safe and secure under the protection of a mighty supernatural force.

When we know this to be true and realize that our safety and security are in the care of the Lord, we can enjoy true peace of mind. Every believer should live in a state of total peace of mind, and this can be accomplished when the spirit of fear vanishes. We also know that we are safe from the condemnation of Hell and from the fear of death, two things that torment many other people.

"HAPPY ART THOU"

When our lives are set apart unto God, we understand the words of Moses when he said to the people of Israel, "Happy art thou":

> Happy art thou, O Israel: who is like unto thee, O people saved by the LORD, the shield of thy help, and who is the sword of thy excellency! and thine enemies shall be found liars unto thee; and thou shalt tread upon their high places.   Deuteronomy 33:29

God is God, and so He provides all our needs, but He is also Lord, and so He rules over us. In order to rule over us, He sets us apart unto Himself, and thereby we are sanctified unto Him to become His peculiar treasure. With such a God and Lord, we have every reason to be full of joy and always happy.

A HAPPY MAN OR WOMAN REJOICES IN THE LORD

During the years that I ministered to Wendy in her sickness, I was conscious of the fact that one of my greatest responsibilities to her was rejoicing in the Lord in her presence. For instance, I sang songs unto the Lord, and each day a certain song became our theme for that day. One such song was this:

Chorus:
Have faith in God,
Have faith in God,
Have faith in God for deliverance,
Have Faith in God.

Faith in God can move a mighty mountain,
Faith in God can calm the troubled seas.
Faith can change the desert to a fountain.
Faith will bring the victory.

Again, our security comes from the fact that we are safe and free from fear because of our God. The answer is to be found in the promises of His Word. Moses declared to the children of Israel that their happiness and safety was in the Lord who brought them out of bondage.

The manifestation of happiness is rejoicing. This the believer does through the singing of psalms, hymns and what the Bible calls *"spiritual songs"* (Ephesians 5:19 and Colossians 3:16).

Our protection is a shield that the supernatural God places over each of us, a covering and a defense for each individual child of God. When we know what the source of our defense is and know how that defense has been demonstrated in past battles and deliverance for the people of God, we can have full assurance. Our Lord is able, and in His faithfulness we can rest assured. This is where the confidence of every child of God originates.

A believer's shield is the righteousness and holiness of God. Plus, we have a two-edged sword, God's Word, that is able to protect us from every fiery dart of the wicked. Paul wrote to his spiritual son Timothy:

For the which cause I also suffer these things: nevertheless I am not ashamed: for I know whom I have believed, and am persuaded that he is able to keep that which I have committed unto him against that day.

2 Timothy 1:12

Children who grow up under the protection and provision of a good father know what it means to feel safe and secure, and this contributes to a very happy childhood. Such children know someone they can always trust, someone they can go to in time of need, and someone they can be assured will provide for them. This is the very kind of happiness we can have in knowing our God.

This is exactly what Moses was seeking to convey to the children of Israel. They could have complete confidence in God's ability to do whatever was necessary for their welfare, and that brought them great joy. After many hundreds of years, they were now free from bondage. And the same God who gave them their freedom would not fail to provide their daily needs.

A CONFIDENT HAPPINESS

In the final years of her life, Wendy had a confident happiness that was the result of her life of holiness and consecration. She happily pronounced to us, "The Lord revealed that I'm going to a better place." That's the confidence we all need.

Paul said he knew in whom he had believed. How about you? Will your faith hold steady for eternity?

Wendy Roberts knew the source of true happiness, and you can too.

Are we alone in our quest for happiness? Never! *Never Alone!* ✳

Chapter 14

SHE WAS WHOLLY CONSECRATED TO GOD

As obedient children, not fashioning yourselves according to the former lusts in your ignorance: but as he which hath called you is holy, so be ye holy in all manner of conversation; because it is written, Be ye holy; for I am holy. 1 Peter 1:14-16

Wendy was wholly consecrated to God, and holiness pleases Him.

Through justification we are guaranteed the divine right through the blood of Jesus Christ. As an heir to eternal life, our sins are washed away, and our names are written in the Lamb's Book of Life. We then become partakers of the divine nature and stand in the righteousness of Jesus Christ, through the work of the cross. This gives us the right to all that God has promised in His covenant of grace.

ACCEPT AND OBEY

When it comes to consecration and salvation, the truth of the Gospel is the responsibility of the hearers to accept and obey. There is no other way to achieve the objective of sanctification, except through the means of God's Word and the work of the Holy Spirit.

Jesus prayed:

They are not of the world, even as I am not of the world. Sanctify them through thy truth: thy word is truth.   John 17:16-17

We must bear in mind that there is no other way to eternal life except through Jesus Christ and no other way to achieve the accepted standard of sanctification except through obedience to His Word, which is truth. The idea that consecration and salvation are somehow an option is foolish. Because of the nature of the Gospel, however, each man or woman, boy or girl is responsible to accept and believe it. Those who refuse will be held accountable.

After this great miracle of salvation occurs, God next commands the believer to be holy. A true believer in Christ can never stand still. Consecration or sanctification is an ongoing process. Whenever the believer stands still or moves in reverse, he becomes a liability to the work of God.

NEVER GO BACKWARD

When Paul wrote his letter to the Colossians, Demas, one of his companions, was in good standing:

> *Luke, the beloved physician, and Demas, greet you.*
>
> Colossians 4:14

At this point, it is clear that Demas' faith was strong, but later on, something happened. Paul wrote to Timothy:

> *For Demas hath forsaken me, having loved this present world, and is departed unto Thessalonica; Crescens to Galatia, Titus unto Dalmatia. Only Luke is with me.*
>
> 2 Timothy 4:10-11

We must bear in mind that there is no other way to eternal life except through Jesus Christ!

When any believer loses his focus on Christ, he tends to drift back toward the world. The enemy of our souls is subtle and continues to use any and all deceptions against us to lure us back to his control.

NEVER ALONE!

When deception has overcome a Christian, he goes back into the kingdom of darkness from which he was once delivered. There he again submits in allegiance to a former master, and once again becomes a slave of the devil. It was for this reason that John wrote to the early Church:

> *Love not the world, neither the things that are in the world. If any man love the world, the love of the Father is not in him. For all that is in the world, the lust of the flesh, and the lust of the eyes, and the pride of life, is not of the Father, but is of the world. And the world passeth away, and the lust thereof: but he that doeth the will of God abideth for ever.*
>
> 1 John 2:15-17

According to the apostle Paul, Demas took a wrong turn, and it cost him his eternal inheritance. We know from the words of Jesus that it will not profit a man to gain the whole world and yet lose his soul (see Matthew 16:26).

The holiness of Paul delivered him from falling into the same trap Demas fell into. What could have happened to Demas? We can make some speculations based on actual experience, and we will probably be right with one or more of these spiritual assumptions:

1. He may have failed to continue in fellowship with believers (forsaking the assembly with the saints of the local church body).

150

2. He may have begun to rely on past experiences and thus lost the joy and delight of seeking the face of God in prayer and intercession.

3. He may not have trusted in the Lord with all his heart, but leaned on his own understanding. Trusting self is the philosophy of a fool, according to the wise Solomon (see Proverbs 28:26).

4. He may have made decisions without the benefit of the wisdom of mature Spirit-filled leaders.

5. He may have lusted after the present world and not sought deliverance through available and powerful men of God.

6. He may have hidden the truth about himself and put up a facade of deceit.

Once we are in the process of sanctification, our love for Jesus is strengthened through the work of the Holy Spirit. We have a love for Jesus that we've never had before. Here's a song to remember that can show us what happens to a Spirit-filled believer in His day-by-day fellowship with the Lord:

> *Every day with Jesus*
> *Is sweeter than the day before.*
> *Every day with Jesus*
> *I love Him more and more.*
> *Jesus saves and keeps me,*
> *And He's the one I'm waiting for.*
> *Every day with Jesus*
> *Is sweeter than the day before.*

Holiness takes away the love we had for the world, and the taste of worldly pleasure is lost forever. Wendy became content in her sanctification through the simple principle of Gospel obedience. Through two years of affliction, there was a genuine reflection of the grace and fruits of the Holy Spirit in her life. The holiness that is required to be in the presence of God, was God's objective, and she moved steadily toward it.

Again, sanctification is not an option; God demands it. Since holiness is a command, those who do not obey the command must face the consequences of disobedience.

The divine benefits of Gospel holiness and Gospel obedience are a closer and closer walk with God. And a closer walk with God demands responsibility and accountability. The conviction of God's Spirit speaks much faster to us the closer we walk with God. As the Holy Spirit ministers to us, we gratefully minister to others.

When someone says, with assurance, that they're going to a better place, as Paul said, that's enough testimony to let the listener know that the Holy Spirit is doing a work of sanctification in them beyond our imagination. He will do the same in our lives when God has determined that we have finished our course here below.

Wendy Roberts was wholly consecrated to God, and you should be too.

Until we have all finished our course here, do we have to go it alone? Never! *Never Alone!*   ✳

PART III

FACING THE FUTURE ALONE

CHAPTER 15

WHAT NOW?

I say therefore to the unmarried and widows, It is good for them if they abide even as I. But if they cannot contain, let them marry: for it is better to marry than to burn. 1 Corinthians 7:8-9

So, like it or not, a whole new chapter was beginning in my life. What would I do with it? Many who lose a loved one in this way fall into deep depression and anxiously await the arrival of death. Some even hasten it by taking their own lives or neglecting their health. They just don't care anymore. They seem to have nothing to live for.

But that can't be right. At the very least, we have some preparing of our own to do for eternity, and for many, years remain to work here in the Lord's harvest.

NEVER ALONE!

OUR FIRST CONCERN

In everything, our first concern must be to please the Lord. It was that way before we married, and it must be that way afterward. Our Lord calls us higher:

> But as he which hath called you is holy, so be ye holy in all manner of conversation; Because it is written, Be ye holy; for I am holy.   1 Peter 1:15-16

> *In everything, our first concern must be to please the Lord!*

Jesus Himself said:

> Be ye therefore perfect, even as your Father which is in heaven is perfect.   Matthew 5:48

Hopefully our marriage has not been a hindrance to holiness. Moses was a married man, and he spent more time in the presence of God than any other of his time. In our text verse, however, we see that the apostle Paul encourages those who are able to live the life-style of one who is single to do so. There are many benefits, he declares, to being single. A single person can do things a married person cannot.

For one, there is the difference in the amount of time available to attend to the things of the Lord. Single people have more time to do what God calls them to do. There are, however, struggles that we must be aware of.

THE STRUGGLES OF THE CONSECRATED WIDOW OR WIDOWER

Those of us who have lost a mate know the struggles that accompany that loss. The oneness that we enjoyed with another human being over many years has suddenly been ripped apart by death, and in order to go on functioning as God intended us to, we need a miracle.

Now instead of being filled with joy, we find ourselves filled with grief. This is a spirit that has to go. The longer we allow it to remain with us, the longer we face the possibility of long-term emotional injury. But we can't just stop remembering, so, what can we do?

If God took from us our ability to hold memories, we would also lose our ability to hold His Word in our hearts, and we need to remember His words. Now, as never before, we have to hide it in our hearts. As it was to David, it is *"a lamp unto my feet, and a light unto my path"* (Psalm 119:105). It must, therefore, remain locked away in our memories. But, alas, along with it are some of the not-so-pleasant memories, those that we wish would go away. Can we do anything about it?

We can. We have control over our minds, to deal with imaginations and thoughts that spring up from our flesh. We deal with such thoughts by using God's Word and speaking it out. It is, after all, the Sword of the Spirit, and the Spirit has the ability to change negative thoughts into a positive reality and joyful scenes and experiences that can help us resist the devil's intentions, the reason he has attacked our minds in the first place. The Word thus spoken can destroy as yet unspoken thoughts.

Tears, Worship and Surrender

When we have loved someone and lived together with them for so long, it is inevitable that the pain of separation and the tears it produces will come to us. That's normal. The question is how long will it last? Will we get over it? That's where we need the Lord's help.

There are certainly times when we wish the mental and emotional anguish of loss would just go away, and the sad thing is that some never recover. Their grieving becomes a spirit that lingers on much too long, maybe the rest of their lives. Although those of us who love the Lord are not exempt from this suffering, if we trust Him, there will come a day when the grief has passed. Where it has gone, we won't really know, but we will know that it's gone, and we can begin to move on with our lives.

Holding on to Precious Memories

One of the things that can help us over this very difficult period is immersing ourselves in the work of the Gospel. As we look back over the years of our ministry together, we can feel a sense of accomplishment. We feel joy because of the contribution we've been able to make. And now we focus even more on fulfilling the command of Jesus:

Go ye therefore, and teach all nations, baptizing them in the name of the Father, and of the Son, and of the Holy Ghost: teaching them to observe all things what-soever I have commanded you: and, lo, I am with you alway, even unto the end of the world. Amen.

Matthew 28:19-20

Feeding those who are hungry is one of our respon-sibilities. We don't have to blow a trumpet every time we do it. Our objective is not to draw attention to our-selves, but to meet the needs of people and thus fulfill the commission of Jesus.

When Jesus fed the four thousand and then the five thousand, He was demonstrating a principle of minis-try, as well as proving by a supernatural sign that He was God and Messiah. He was setting an example for us to show compassion to those who are in need. When we do that, our acts should bring Him glory, and we must never boast of what we have done. If doing God's work causes us to fall into pride, that is very sad in-deed.

Always remember that our God, who is omniscient, or all-knowing, has already recorded the works that we have done and are even now doing in His Name. We remember them, and it brings joy and comfort to our souls. Just to know that we have been used by God is fulfilling in itself. We rejoice in being used by Him to carry the message of the Gospel to the poor.

Jesus taught:

Then shall the righteous answer him, saying, Lord, when saw we thee an hungered, and fed thee? or thirsty, and gave thee drink? When saw we thee a stranger, and took thee in? or naked, and clothed thee? Or when saw we thee sick, or in prison, and came unto thee? And the King shall answer and say unto them, Verily I say unto you, Inasmuch as ye have done it unto one of the least of these my brethren, ye have done it unto me. Matthew 25:37-40

A BEAUTIFUL LIFE AHEAD

There is a beautiful life ahead for every consecrated widow or widower. When the Lord has called home one partner to receive their reward for a life of dedication, consecration and faithfulness to Him, there is a great inventory of resources that He has planted in the heart and mind of the partner who is left behind, and this can bring joy and peace to those who will, in the future, experience what has transpired in your life.

The strength of recovery and the return of joy where there was once nothing but sorrow will be a testimony for others to see, and they, in turn, will be encouraged to face the unknown future with faith and confidence. God is *"able to keep that which [we] have committed unto him"*:

For the which cause I also suffer these things: nevertheless I am not ashamed: for I know whom I have believed, and am persuaded that he is able to keep that which I have committed unto him against that day.
2 Timothy 1:12

RESOURCES FOR RECOVERY

The resources for comfort and recovery come from various sources. Family and friends and the saints with whom we fellowship will be a wonderful source of joy to us. There is a core group that will make themselves available when you need them. There are co-workers and members of various organizations that you were members with who will be willing to lend support and encouragement. In my case, many who worked in the ministry of evangelism with me through the years were available to help me now. Pastors and church leaders, who were partners in the ministry of evangelism, were present. Those who had experienced what I had gone through could understand. I am sure of one truth: Jesus understands.

Am I alone? Well, sometimes it does feel like it, but we know that this is not the case. Those of us who are in Christ are *Never Alone!* ✳

CHAPTER 16

REMARRYING?

Be careful for nothing; but in every thing by prayer and supplication with thanksgiving let your requests be made known unto God. And the peace of God ... shall keep your hearts and minds through Christ Jesus.
Philippians 4:6-7

Consecrated widows and widowers, as well as single people, must find the perfect plan of God for their lives. This might include remaining single for life, or God, in His sovereign will, may answer their prayer in a very different way, reserving a special someone for them. God has a consecrated husband for every woman called to be a consecrated wife, a consecrated wife for every man called to be a consecrated husband, and He knows where that special someone lives. In fact, He saw them even before the foundations of the world.

It's never your job to find your prospective spouse and then save them. That's the responsibility of the Holy Spirit. He finds them, and then He calls them by His Spirit, and when that is accomplished, He positions both of you in the place where He wants you to meet. When all of this is in place, only then can He bring you together.

Every single saint destined to marry should expect to find their predestined mate in the place God has ordained for their first meeting. When it happens, you will see each other with eyes of faith and wonder. This is not to say that you are meeting for the very first time. You may well have seen each other before, but then God had not placed the mantel of His love in your spirits.

The Bible tells us about the day Isaac first laid eyes on Rebekah:

And Isaac went out to meditate in the field at the eventide: and he lifted up his eyes, and saw, and, behold, the camels were coming. And Rebekah lifted up her eyes, and when she saw Isaac, she lighted off the camel. And Isaac brought her into his mother Sarah's tent, and took Rebekah, and she became his wife; and he loved her: and Isaac was comforted after his mother's death. Genesis 24:63-64 and 67

Marriage has the power to heal the brokenhearted and comfort those who are in great distress and sorrow, but marriage should be consummated only when two people find their partner in a spirit of joy. There are times when marriage can heal emotional stresses that no other remedy could alleviate. This is why it is important to live a sanctified life. That way you will be ready when God reveals your intended mate.

Isaac was waiting, and yet he found time to meditate in the field at eventide. He was seeking peace and assurance in Jehovah. In such a time of waiting and grief, there is no better way to spend an evening than to meditate on God. He, in turn, by His Holy Spirit, brings comfort to our souls.

Every single saint destined to marry should expect to find their predestined mate in the place God has ordained for their first meeting!

THE FIRST TIME HE EVER SAW HER FACE

Without ever having seen her, Isaac instinctively knew that this was a God-sent bride. The only explanation for such a thing must be that the Spirit revealed it to him. And that's the very best way. When the Holy Spirit gives us a witness, there remains no doubt in our hearts. What is this "witness"? There is something in the human spirit that tells a believer when a blessing is divine, the work of God. You just somehow know that what has been revealed is perfect for you.

We all have our memories of the first time we met and the last time we were together, and these will remain with us forever. As I noted early on, I first met Wendy at the Goldwater Memorial Hospital in New York City. We were both working there, ministering to the sick. We met in April, and four months later, after searching our hearts for the will of God for our lives, we consummated the marriage.

That year, 1976, marked the beginning of our thirty-one year partnership in the work of the Lord Jesus Christ. We were part of the ministry of the International Crusaders for Christ, and part of our commission was to preach the Gospel to those who were confined in wheelchairs. Although our primary concern was to see men and women come to Christ and be saved, God also demonstrated His power to heal, confirming His Word. One patient walked out of that hospital and was able to go back home and resume her normal life. Praise the Lord, He still heals the sick today. And through this ministry, we met.

WHERE IS MY BELOVED?

The man or woman you are looking for should not be somewhere sitting idly, waiting. They should be occupied doing something constructive. A consecrated man or woman of God is never idle. This is an important sign that can let you know who may be Mr. or Ms. Right, appointed by God, and who is definitely not. Your man or woman may be part of a prayer team, a member of a Gospel choir or already on some mission field, preaching or teaching the Word of God.

When we are single and truly saved, we have a love for Jesus that causes us to want to please Him and Him only. All of our time is dedicated to giving Christ the best. When a person is consumed with the natural fulfillment of their desires and loneliness, they often grab at the first sign of an available mate, and then they search for reasons to justify what they have done, hoping all the while that everything will work out.

But this is a tragic mistake. When we say that we trust the Lord, and yet we're not willing to wait on Him in something as important as this, then it becomes evident that we are using eyes of flesh.

We must never forget what happened to Samson when he used eyes of flesh. What he saw caused him to make a disastrous choice. The problem is that our eyes of flesh can only see the outward appearance. It takes the eyes of the Spirit to see in a way not normal to man.

When the prophet Samuel was sent to find and anoint a king for Israel, God warned him about using eyes of flesh:

But the LORD said unto Samuel, Look not on his countenance, or on the height of his stature; because I have refused him: for the LORD seeth not as man seeth; for man looketh on the outward appearance, but the LORD looketh on the heart. 1 Samuel 16:7

167

The reason this is so important is that it takes a man with a heart after God to do the type of service necessary to fulfill the biblical ideal of marriage, a demonstration of the love between Christ and His Church (see Ephesians 5:23-25), and the same is true of the woman. This means that in times when sickness such as the cancer that is touching the lives of many believers, there will be enough love in our hearts and enough determination in our spirits to remain consistent in patience and service, as a child of God must be, and to do it with all our heart and soul. In such times, we cannot afford to give in to the spirit of discouragement.

A consecrated man or woman, filled with the Holy Ghost, is under spiritual restraints to focus on the cross!

A consecrated man or woman, filled with the Holy Ghost, is under spiritual restraints to focus on the cross. They begin to know how to take up the cross of discipline and seek to walk in the Spirit in order to avoid the impulses of the flesh. They leave the job at the end of their workday and head home to spend time with their Lord in prayer and the study of His Word. There is no room in their life for "hanging out" with friends or going to ungodly places. Always remember what the Word of God tells us:

This I say then, Walk in the Spirit, and ye shall not fulfil the lust of the flesh. For the flesh lusteth against the Spirit, and the Spirit against the flesh: and these are contrary the one to the other: so that ye cannot do the things that ye would. Galatians 5:16-17

This is a word that the Lord desires every consecrated believer to keep in their heart, so that they might not sin against their God. Remember that *"your body is the temple of the Holy Ghost"* (1 Corinthians 6:19). Our eyes of flesh always attempt to bring scenes to the mind that have the potential to damn our very souls. The devil's tools are still the same. He deceived Eve by getting her to look, while he talked smoothly into her ear.

A truly consecrated man or woman of God heads home to their loved ones. Thus, they will never stray into some Satan-directed pleasure. Such temptation is easily resisted, as they walk in the consecration of the Holy Spirit.

Friends, live holy, because God is Holy, and He demands us to live holy. How can we do that? We do it through the abiding presence of His Spirit. This is not a heavy burden. The psalmist declared:

Thy word have I hid in mine heart, that I might not sin against thee. Psalm 119:11

The Word of God in our hearts serves as a constant reminder and raises a red flag of warning when we are heading toward danger. When the Spirit says, "STOP

NOW and go back to the path of life and deliverance," obey. Go no further. If you insist on doing otherwise, you are headed for disaster.

The Holy Spirit is faithful, and His work is to convict us. If we refuse Him, then God will not tolerate our stiffnecked rebellion, for He has done so much for us and promised us so much in the future. What a Savior!

Again, the psalmist declared:

Thy word is a lamp unto my feet, and a light unto my path.   Psalm 119:105

As we faithfully follow His lead, He will show us His perfect will for us, the single life, or someone special to share it with. The choice is not based on whether one person is better than another, but that the eventual partner is God's choice and His best for you. So just trust Him.

In the meantime, are you alone? It may feel like it sometimes, but know that you are really not alone. *Never Alone!*   ✻

CHAPTER 17

THE ROLE OF DATING AND COURTSHIP

But if any man think that he behaveth himself uncomely toward his virgin, if she pass the flower of her age, and need so require, let him do what he will, he sinneth not: let them marry.
[But] only in the Lord.   1 Corinthians 7:36 and 39

What is the proper role of dating and courtship in the Christian life? Let me ask this: Who brought dating into the sanctified Church in the first place? It certainly wasn't the apostle Paul. Dating is part of the Western culture and part of apostate Christendom. Dating and courtship are not and never have been Christian customs. And this is not just my opinion; it's the Gospel truth.

Dating was never condoned by God in Old Testament times, and neither was it ever introduced as part of the New Covenant. Why, then, should two holy and Spirit-filled Christians follow the world's system, with all of its filth, and start dating? If you are in the will of God for His glory and pleasure, then leave out all the foolishness and just do as Paul has said: *"Let them marry!"*

> *When you know the will of God, why waste precious time looking like the world and acting like the heathen around you?*

WHY WASTE PRECIOUS TIME?

When you know the will of God, why waste precious time looking like the world and acting like the heathen around you? And if you do date, how could you then think that you're still shining as *"the light of the world"* (Matthew 5:14) for the sake of Christ?

Courtship and dating for Christians is using carnal preparation for what amounts to a spiritual battle. No wonder so many marriages fail these days!

I speak from the experience of a successful thirty-one year marriage, and it was successful because it was founded on the rock of prayer and built using the materials of truth. We didn't have to date to know the will of God.

In Bible days, Joseph didn't "date" Mary. He was *"espoused"* to her (Luke 1:27), meaning that they were pledged to be married. Such a pledge, covenant or agreement was made between parties to enter into marriage at some specified future date, but that didn't give them license to then start "fooling around." Marriage was seen as a serious responsibility, and the concerned parties immediately entered into a period of deep spiritual preparation. They didn't have time to waste on all the secular and carnal organizing that has become so expensive and time consuming in our day.

Before any marriage is entered into, there should always be a period of waiting and praying, so that each partner can be satisfied of the will of God for their lives together. It is not possible to find this will out on a date, sipping wine together or cheating on your vows. The will of God is only revealed through prayer and earnest commitment to intercession. Marriage is an awesome responsibility, and it requires an equally awesome preparation.

UNCOVERING A COUNTERFEIT PARTNER

During such a time of prayer, some may discover that their intended partner is not what he or she at first appeared to be:

And Nadab and Abihu, the sons of Aaron, took either of them his censer, and put fire therein, and put in-

cense thereon, and offered strange fire before the L{\sc ord}, which he commanded them not. And there went out fire from the L{\sc ord}, and devoured them, and they died before the L{\sc ord}. Then Moses said unto Aaron, This is it that the L{\sc ord} spake, saying, I will be sanctified in them that come nigh me, and before all the people I will be glorified. And Aaron held his peace.

Leviticus 10:1-3

These two sons of Aaron looked like holy priests, but they couldn't fool God. His Holy Spirit revealed the strange fire in their hands, and they were judged because of it. Nothing is covered, or hidden, with God.

This same sensitivity is needed by those who are contemplating marriage. Appearances, very often, can be deceiving. God, by His Spirit, can raise some red flags to tip you off before it's too late. Nothing could be more important for those seeking a partner for life.

Don't be afraid to put your potential partner to the test. See how comfortable they are in the powerful presence of the Holy Ghost. It is often possible to then determine if theirs is a fervent desire for the deeper things of God, or if it is just a shallow or weak commitment which could never handle the kinds of battles and fierce attacks that very commonly come against marriages today.

Marriage is a decision for a lifetime, and so it's not wrong to put it to the acid test. Praying and waiting before God will uncover any deception or counterfeit profession of Christian faith.

A PERFECT EXAMPLE

There are many glaring examples all around us. In order not to offend anyone, I will leave out the names in this perfect example: Mr. Not Right and Ms. Not Right dated for three years and did everything Western society endorses. Then, they got married, but within just a few years, the marriage came crashing down.

In a contrasting case, Mr. Righteous Right and Ms. Holy Right had their first encounter on the mission field. They were both Spirit-filled believers. They were drawn to each other, but they decided to complete their education and then find proper employment before marrying. In the meantime, their relationship grew, but it was based on truth and facts, not mere emotions or hormones. By the time they felt they were ready for marriage, this couple had fulfilled all their God-ordained requirements for partnership for life. They had no regrets to overcome, and they went on to serve out the years of their partnership together in perfect harmony and joy. Theirs was a testimony of how obedience and submission to the will of God produces victory and prosperity every time.

You, too, need to fulfill all spiritual prerequisites and not be afraid to apply every important acid test when you are contemplating a life together in marriage. Let the Holy Spirit guide you. He is *"a discerner of the thoughts and intents of the heart"* (Hebrews 4:12).

Paul wrote to the Romans:

Therefore, brethren, we are debtors, not to the flesh, to live after the flesh. For if ye live after the flesh, ye shall die: but if ye through the Spirit do mortify the deeds of the body, ye shall live. For as many as are led by the Spirit of God, they are the sons of God.

Romans 8:12-14

Everyone who is saved should recognize the need to marry another child of God. No one intends to marry a child of the devil, and yet it happens. When Christians make this mistake, they are prone to trivialize it and try to make the best of a bad situation. In time, however, the demons do surface, and then all Hell breaks loose.

Here is a partner's checklist that could be helpful for those looking for a proper mate:

A PARTNER'S CHECKLIST

☐ Is this person saved?
☐ Is this person filled with the Holy Spirit?
☐ Has this person completed the necessary educational objectives?
☐ Has this person committed their life to the Lord for service?
☐ Is this person aware that they were created for God's pleasure (see Revelation 4:11)?

A DATING QUESTION

Some pastors give young people advice based on their personal opinion, but that doesn't necessarily make it right in the eyes of God. For example, here's a probing question: Should Christian young people go to the movies together, for entertainment and relaxation, so that they can get to know their prospective life partner better? Is that the kind of place Christian young people should go for this purpose?

There's no easy answer to the question. If you could take the hand of Jesus and lead Him into that place and He would willingly go, then it may be okay. If Jesus were to say, "This is in line with all My teachings on Christian discipleship and conduct," then, by all means, go. But if He would not be happy with what is being viewed there or the type of crowd that is commonly seen there, then why would you want to go there for any reason?

If Jesus were to say, "This is in line with all My teachings on Christian discipleship and conduct," then, by all means, go!

God walked and talked with Adam, having sweet fellowship with him in the garden, and that's what He wants to do with you too. If you have to leave Him outside of the places you frequent, then you're making a mistake by going there.

Many seem to have the idea that they can have it both ways. They leave God outside and go have their "fun," and then they think they can pick Him back up again on their way home and enjoy His blessings in their lives. This is living a double life, and it is nothing more than hypocrisy.

THE PURPOSE OF MARRIAGE IN THE EYES OF GOD

From the Holy Scriptures, we can find God's divine plan for marriage. When a man and woman marry, they are entrusting their future into the hands of the Almighty. The Lord will control the number of offspring they bear, and He will supply all their needs. We are created for God's glory and pleasure:

> *Thou art worthy, O Lord, to receive glory and honour and power: for thou hast created all things, and for thy pleasure they are and were created.*
>
> Revelation 4:11

There is power in a consecrated life, and there is even more power in a consecrated marriage. Every couple seeking a wonderful and excellent life must first begin with Christ as their foundation. A marriage built on a weak foundation will not stand in difficult times. Begin with a strong foundation, and you will be assured of victory with each new day.

FEELINGS OF LOVE WITHOUT TRUTH IS A DISASTER

The blending of two lives for a lifetime must be based on truth and love. We know that often our first impressions of each other is based on physical appearance. This is true for both sexes. But only the Holy Spirit can see what is in the heart. There are often secrets that cannot be seen by the eyes of man.

Here are some things that commonly catch our attention about another person:

- Their eyes
- Their smile
- Their height
- Their age
- The color of their skin
- Their weight
- Their general body language
- Their mannerisms and speech
- Their race
- Their religion

But none of these can tell who a person really is. This is why the benefit of "love at first sight" is limited. I'm not saying that such a union cannot work out to be a lasting partnership, but I am saying that we cannot base our future on looks or feelings of love. It must be based on truth.

NEVER ALONE!

Think of the great judge of Israel, Samson, again. It was feelings of love that destroyed him. Truth could have set him free if he had allowed it to happen. Instead, the chains of a love gone wrong imprisoned him, and his end was very sad.

Truth must be your guide, and the feelings of love must be a much less important consideration!

We know that the devil is the archenemy of the Church and of Christ. He seeks to destroy any man or woman who has the potential for ministry. He seeks to destroy every young person whom God has placed His hands on. This is the reason that truth must be your guide, and the feelings of love must be a much less important consideration. Feelings of love have sometimes blinded the eyes of very wise people.

If even a consecrated man can be blinded by feelings of love, then that shows how important it is to be guided by truth. This is the only way we can successfully avoid the traps set by the devil for us.

Sometimes the feeling of love can be so overwhelming that those who experience it come to believe that it somehow changes truth. When this happens, truth can be staring them in the face, but they're so consumed with the feelings of love and what they want out of their love experience that they actually deceive themselves. "Surely such a powerful love can overcome any obstacle," they think. But those obstacles they are pushing aside are actually their present reality.

They're so in love that they're sure the future will be okay. She pleases him, and he pleases her. What could possibly go wrong? But those were the very thoughts of Samson, and still his ministry came crashing down.

LOVE GROWS, FALLS OR DIES; TRUTH REMAINS THE SAME FOREVER

Feelings of love can grow or change, but truth is ever-lasting, and it stands forever. It is more comfortable to trust in something that never changes, and the feeling of love does change over time. It sometimes grows stronger, but it also sometimes grows weaker. It never stays the same. It can sometimes surprise and delight us, and it can sometimes disappoint and hurt us.

Real love comes because of truth. It is truth that gives us the freedom and the confidence to love. When every-thing is in line with the truth, then love can grow to its highest potential. And a simple acid test of truth can de-stroy every lie set to harm the innocent. When an innocent lamb is in the embrace of the deceiver, truth is the only power that can give that lamb the power to es-cape to freedom and peace and life.

TRUTH WILL NEVER DIE

Truth feeds true love. When love gets its nourishment

from truth, it grows and flourishes. In our world today, how can a marriage last for thirty-one years? We not only survived; we survived with an abundance of love and joy. Truth nourished our togetherness, and we embraced that truth with delight.

Truth never dies, but when love is a lie, it will die and leave in its path misery and pain. These final paragraphs were added to this chapter as a warning to those who may feel that they know it all. Please stop at the crossroads of truth and follow the arrow that says, *"Ye shall know the truth, and the truth shall make you free"* (John 8:32).

TRUTH REJECTED: A TRUE STORY

I knew two very hard-working and seemingly success-ful professionals who were both at an age in which marriage seemed to be passing them by. A matchmaker brought them together, and before long they "fell in love" and began dating. That may sound like the beginning of a wonderful story, but the end of this particular story is very sad.

Before long, both of these very successful profession-als began failing to complete their assigned projects. Oh, someone else was always to blame, but it happened over and over again. In the end, they failed at everything they attempted and always had someone to blame for it.

Eventually, they backslid into a powerless, nominal Christian life. Still they could not imagine that they had done anything to cause it. As always, it was someone else's fault.

THE DEVIL IS A WICKED MATCHMAKER

The point I want to make here should be clear. Our concept is that feelings of love will conquer all, but when truth is rejected, then what we call "love" actually becomes destructive. These two seemingly successful professionals should have seen, from the very beginning, the failure of the testimony of their chosen life partner. Each of them was a quitter, and quitters never accomplish anything. Their pattern of life revealed the truth, but no one wanted to look hard enough to see it. Please don't base your marriage on such a shaky foundation.

These two young people trusted in their own hearts, and now they are suffering the consequences of rejecting the truth. Eventually the crash came, and along with it came the pain, the rejection and the disappointment. Again, when you're at the crossroads of truth and doubt, be sure to take the right turn.

So, in seeking a proper mate for life, know that you are not alone. *Never Alone!* ✳

CHAPTER 18

AWAITING OUR OWN "WELL DONE!"

Then shall the righteous answer him, saying, Lord, when saw we thee an hungered, and fed thee? or thirsty, and gave thee drink? Matthew 25:37

Well done! What do those words mean? Millions will hear them spoken as they stand before God, for they will stand in the righteousness of Jesus Christ. What joy will permeate the atmosphere at that moment!

However, billions will never hear those welcome words from the Righteous Judge of all the earth. Instead, they will stand before Him with not a single word of defense, and all the angels of Heaven will be there to bear witness to that fact. These will have chosen the broad way that leads to death, and they will have eternity to regret their foolish decision:

Enter ye in at the strait gate: for wide is the gate, and broad is the way, that leadeth to destruction, and many there be which go in thereat: because strait is the gate, and narrow is the way, which leadeth unto life, and few there be that find it. Matthew 7:13-14

The Holy Spirit is God's Intelligent Agent, and it's not possible for believers to do stupid things when they depend on Him. It does happen, but if we depend on His intelligence and desire to obey Him without reservation, we can escape many of the pitfalls of life.

If we do depend upon the Holy Spirit, we can please God. I know that everything that I do must be well done. We already know the predetermined judgment, what Jesus Himself will say to us, in recognition of what we have done—well or not.

We Can Know Whether a Thing Is Well Done or Not

1. To be well done, the work that we do must be done thoroughly and carefully and in a satisfactory manner. There must be no motive of "what's in it for me." The motive for what we do must never include selfish thought. At the end of our mission, we have to say that we are *"unprofitable servants"*:

So likewise ye, when ye shall have done all those things which are commanded you, say, We are unprofitable servants: we have done that which was our duty to do. Luke 17:10

2. We must have no earthly "stake" in the Gospel. At no time must a servant use God's work as a means of making an earthly profit:

Then Peter said, Silver and gold have I none; but such as I have give I thee: In the name of Jesus Christ of Nazareth rise up and walk. And he took him by the right hand, and lifted him up: and immediately his feet and ankle bones received strength. Acts 3:6-7

> *At no time must a servant use God's work as a means of making an earthly profit!*

We cannot use the manifestations of God's blessings or deliverance to further our own well-being. This confuses the people of the world as to the motives of a servant of God. Peter gave all the glory to Jesus alone.

"GREATLY BELOVED" VS. "WELL DONE"

Daniel received the commendation *"well done"* in an-

other way. An angel said that he was *"greatly beloved."*
This shows that this servant's work was done with a dedication and a quality of excellence that merited praise:

> *And he said unto me, O Daniel, a man greatly beloved,*
> *understand the words that I speak unto thee, and stand*
> *upright, for unto thee am I now sent. And when he had*
> *spoken this word unto me, I stood trembling.*
> *Then said he unto me, Fear not, Daniel: for from the first*
> *day that thou didst set thine heart to understand, and to*
> *chasten thyself before thy God, thy words were heard,*
> *and I am come for thy words.*   Daniel 10:11-12

How wonderful to hear such words from an angelic
being!

ALL WHO ARE AMONG THE BELOVED?

Daniel was the only person in the Bible to be called
"greatly beloved." Jesus was called, by the Father, *"my be-*
loved Son":

> *And the Holy Ghost descended in a bodily shape like a*
> *dove upon him, and a voice came from heaven, which*
> *said, Thou art my beloved Son; in thee I am well*
> *pleased.*   Luke 3:22

So that was very special. However, all of us who are
believers are included in the biblical term *"the beloved."*
In the Song of Solomon, the word *beloved* is used

thirty-one times, in the husband/wife relationship or as a bridegroom to his bride. When God used the word *beloved,* He was referring to those who serve Him in obedience and holiness for the pleasure of His glory.

Long before the Righteous Judge of all the earth commended Daniel (on the Day of Judgment) He had already said to him that he was *"greatly beloved"* during his lifetime. This was the same as saying to him, "Well done, for unselfish service to your God." It meant that the way he had spent his time on earth was acceptable in the sight of the Almighty.

The Heart of Daniel Was Pure

The heart of every servant who works for Christ must be pure. There must be no secret motives or secret agendas. God will look at us through and through, so the servant of God must live a transparent life.

"Well done" doesn't have anything to do with the size or bigness of the work that we have done for God. It has everything to do with how we commit ourselves to pursue His work in faithfulness and excellence to the best of our abilities. There was integrity in the life of this man of God under the administration of the Holy Spirit.

"Well done," has everything to do with the sincerity of sacrifice that we make unto the Lord. The best belongs to Him, without any desire on our part for boasting of how much we have given to Him as compared to the sacrifice of others.

Daniel Took No Gifts or Rewards for What God Did through Him

Then Daniel answered and said before the king, Let thy gifts be to thyself, and give thy rewards to another; yet I will read the writing unto the king, and make known to him the interpretation.

Daniel 5:17

> *We can know if we are standing on solid or sinking ground!*

There are preachers who take the church offerings and hide it in their pocket. "This is mine," they contend. "I worked for it. Why should I declare it and have to pay taxes on it?" When this happens, money has clearly become the root of an evil heart. Daniel, however, knew that there was a greater reward awaiting him from the King of Kings and the Lord of Lords.

Use This Acid Test To Evaluate Your Life

I have chosen the prophet Daniel in this chapter because he was the only man God called *"greatly beloved,"* but there are many other men and women of God whom we can examine and use as a measuring rod to check our own lives. Thus, we can know if we are standing on solid or sinking ground.

Take, for example, Noah. He was called *"a preacher of righteousness"* (2 Peter 2:5) during the time he was preparing the Ark. He built it with all His strength and skill, just as God had ordered him to. Anything we build for God or any service we render to Him must be according to His design and plan, and not according to any measure of the world's standards.

If a work is not done well, the record of it will be thrown in God's waste basket, to be burned up by His fire. It is a fearful thing to say that we are doing anything for God, if, in truth and in fact, we are actually doing it for ourselves. It is important that we do not run the dangerous, damnable risk of hearing our Lord say, *"I never knew you: depart from me, ye that work iniquity"* (Matthew 7:23).

We must each see that we fulfill the ministry God has given us. We must know what that work is and seek the wisdom of the Holy Spirit as we pursue to fulfill it. If it is received by men, then we are obligated to men, but if it is received by the Lord, we must please Him alone.

This is the work Jesus was talking about when He spoke these words to all men in His Sermon on the Mount:

Not every one that saith unto me, Lord, Lord, shall enter into the kingdom of heaven; but he that doeth the will of my Father which is in heaven. Many will say to me in that day, Lord, Lord, have we not prophesied in thy name? and in thy name have cast out devils? and in thy name done many wonderful works?

NEVER ALONE!

And then will I profess unto them, I never knew you:
depart from me, ye that work iniquity.

Matthew 7:21-23

Try to be a Daniel in your generation, and demon-strate the life of consecration among family, friends and neighbors and, most of all, the poor. These are the little ones whom Jesus called *"my brethren."* Let us live like Daniel, or even better, like Jesus.

DARE TO BE A DANIEL

Standing by a purpose firm,
Heeding God's command
Honor them the faithful few.
All hail to Daniel's band.

Chorus:
Dare to be a Daniel.
Dare to stand alone.
Dare to have a purpose firm.
And dare to make it known.

Many mighty men are lost,
Daring not to stand,
Who for God had been a host,
By joining Daniel's band.

Many giants great and tall,
Stalking through the land,

Headlong to the earth would fall
If met by Daniel's band.

Hold the gospel banner high
In to victory grand.
Satan and his host defy
And shout for Daniel's band.

We should not only sing it; we should live it!

What about your "well done"? When Wendy received her bad news that the cancer returned, her first reaction was, "Why me, Lord?" But before she left this life, she had said two more memorable things: "I have lived a good and godly life" and "He told me that I'm going to a better place." Oh that we can all say these things when our time comes to put off this, our earthly tabernacle!

In the meantime, are we alone? Never! *Never Alone!* ✳

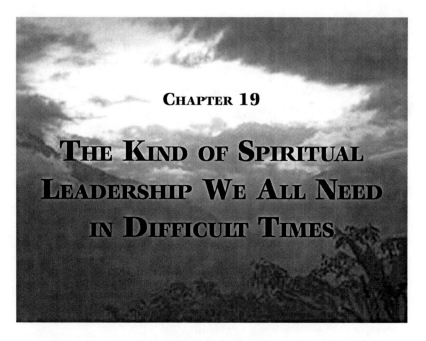

CHAPTER 19

THE KIND OF SPIRITUAL LEADERSHIP WE ALL NEED IN DIFFICULT TIMES

When [Jesus] was come down from the mountain, great multitudes followed him. And, behold, there came a leper and worshipped him, saying, Lord, if thou wilt, thou canst make me clean. And Jesus put forth his hand, and touched him, saying, I will; be thou clean. And immediately his leprosy was cleansed.

Matthew 8:1-3

Today, we have far too many of what I have come to call "pretty-boy" pastors in our churches. They are hirelings who, in reality, care little for the sheep, and the proof is that they never get their hands dirty caring for others. Such hirelings are clearly not much like our Lord Jesus.

195

NEVER ALONE!

Jesus *"touched"* the leper, and in so doing, He demonstrated, that He, the most holy and consecrated One, was willing to reach down to men and women in need in order to lift them up. He ministered not only to those who could reward Him, but to the needy, the poor and the suffering among humanity. They had little to offer in return, but then, that's why He came. He came to give, not to receive.

Jesus ministered not only to those who could reward Him, but to the needy, the poor and the suffering among humanity!

I'm afraid that many of our current pastors are not even concerned with the souls of the lost. Their constant goal is self gratification. They want to be seen, but they have no desire to live a life that is wholesome and pure. May God give us more consecrated men in the pulpit today!

Jesus said:

But he that is an hireling, and not the shepherd, whose own the sheep are not, seeth the wolf coming, and leaveth the sheep, and fleeth: and the wolf catcheth them, and scattereth the sheep. The hireling fleeth, because he is an hireling, and careth not for the sheep. John 10:12-13

There is a veritable famine in the pulpit today, and our need for consecrated men in the ministries has never been greater. It's not enough that we lack men who care about the lost; we even lack men who are available to minister to the consecrated saints and to take them to higher heights in the things of the Spirit. Saints require a constantly increasing nourishment to satisfy the hunger of their souls. To supply such nourishment requires men who are sold out to God and dedicated to the welfare of the entire flock.

The writer to the Hebrews declared:

For every one that useth milk is unskilful in the word of righteousness: for he is a babe. But strong meat belongeth to them that are of full age, even those who by reason of use have their senses exercised to discern both good and evil. Hebrews 5:13-14

I'm very grateful to the Lord that He sent men from thousands of miles away to minister to Wendy's spiritual needs before she went on to be with Jesus. The last time she partook of the Lord's Supper here on earth, it was ministered to her by one of those pastors God had sent. That's how caring and concerned our God is about the details of our lives. Oh, that those who call themselves men of God in this nation would be as caring! God has called us to demonstrate to each other and to the world the thing that makes us unique among all men—the peculiar language of God's love—and that is only done through selfless service.

So many prominent pastors today are considered to have a gift of preaching, but I find their message rather difficult to digest. It's clear to me that their motivation is money. True men of God speak out of deep conviction from the Spirit, and their motives are always pure because Christ is the center of their heart and their work. His commission, to reach the lost, is paramount in their thinking, and the continued development of the members of the Body of Christ until they reach spiritual maturity is always one of their chief goals:

> *Therefore leaving the principles of the doctrine of Christ, let us go on unto perfection; not laying again the foundation of repentance from dead works, and of faith toward God, of the doctrine of baptisms, and of laying on of hands, and of resurrection of the dead, and of eternal judgment.* Hebrews: 6:1-2

Why is all of this so important, and what does it have to do with this book? In times of crisis, we cannot afford to rely on immature Christians. It is only mature believers who can minister truth to us and our loved ones, so that we are spiritually challenged and lifted up in faith to face our trials and continue to fight the good fight of faith. Selfish and self-serving pastors, on the other hand, cannot deliver real spiritual food. They themselves have not been feasting on that spiritual manna.

When Jesus touched the leper, He was setting an example for all those in the future who would call themselves His followers. They would have to humble themselves enough to touch the lepers, reaching down to the poorest of the poor, the weakest of the weak, the sickest of the sick and the most lonely of the lonely.

Wendy knew how to do that. She was never afraid or hesitant to touch the hand of those whom Jesus called "the least of these my brethren." During more than twenty years of caring for and comforting the sick at the Marcus Garvey Nursing Home in Brooklyn, New York, she represented her Lord well. May each of us do the same in the days ahead.

In the meantime, are we alone? Never! *Never Alone!* ✳

CHAPTER 20

CHRIST'S OFFER OF SALVATION

And to you who are troubled rest with us, when the Lord Jesus shall be revealed from heaven with his mighty angels, in flaming fire taking vengeance on them that know not God, and that obey not the gospel of our Lord Jesus Christ ...   2 Thessalonians 1:7-8

I cannot end this book without extending an invitation to the lost and backslidden. In this powerful passage, God is mercifully commanding us to save ourselves from eternal death, and He has also provided the means of our salvation. That is love that cannot be defined. Our only means of expressing such love can be found in the words of John 3:16: *"For God so loved ... ."* How else could we describe His endless mercy and grace?

DEFINING THE PHRASE *So Loved*

The common phrase we use, *so much,* means "a limited measure of a certain item," but these words *so loved* are only limited by the billions of human beings who have existed from Adam to the end of time, for they can all be saved through the shed blood of Jesus Christ. There is enough power in His blood to save anyone and everyone.

This is how vast the love of our God is. This is His amazing grace, even for all the generations not yet born. But only those who come to Him by faith will receive salvation and atonement for their sins.

Salvation and holiness are two commands we are called to obey. The command to obey the Gospel, to the end that we are saved from the condemnation of Hell, is the mercy of a loving and caring God. It's not an option, but a command. So it's a very serious matter that we must each consider, a matter of life and death, a matter of eternal destiny. God expects that those who are entrusted with the preaching of the Gospel of the salvation will accept this most important and awesome truth. Without salvation through the blood of Jesus Christ, no one would be justified to receive the Holy Spirit, which is power to live a holy life and have fellowship with God on a daily basis.

The presentation of the message must have objective truth of God's eternal purpose. Man is responsible to act on the command to believe or be faced with the task of accountability to God for rejecting the truth, the only provision made by God. Disobedient and rebellious man will be held accountable for not believing the record that God gave of His son, the Lord Jesus Christ:

> *Nevertheless I tell you the truth; It is expedient for you that I go away: for if I go not away, the Comforter will not come unto you; but if I depart, I will send him unto you. And when he is come, he will reprove the world of sin, and of righteousness, and of judgment: of sin, because they believe not on me; of righteousness, because I go to my Father, and ye see me no more; of judgment, because the prince of this world is judged.*
>
> John 16:7-11

> *Salvation and holiness are two commands we are called to obey!*

Salvation is God's gift to man for obeying the claims of the Gospel. God will hold every man responsible for rejecting the truth about His Son, the Lord Jesus Christ. We are commanded to repent:

> *Now after that John was put in prison, Jesus came into Galilee, preaching the gospel of the kingdom of God, and saying, The time is fulfilled, and the kingdom of God is at hand: repent ye, and believe the gospel.*
>
> Mark 1:14-15

NEVER ALONE!

For the Christians in a Backslidden Condition

There is a command to repent to escape the condemnation of Hell. Christians who backslide and become cold and lukewarm must take heed, lest they find themselves suffering the same fate as the ungodly:

> *Remember therefore from whence thou art fallen, and repent, and do the first works; or else I will come unto thee quickly, and will remove thy candlestick out of his place, except thou repent.* Revelation 2:5

For Anyone without Christ

Twice in this verse, the word *repent* is used. This means that the emphasis is on the seriousness of the spiritual condition that must be quickly attended to, as God sees the urgency of the restoration back to fellowship with Him. Failure to repent is spiritual ignorance on the part of anyone who does not know Jesus as Savior and Lord. There must be true repentance, which is the prerequisite of obeying the Gospel of God:

> *For the time is come that judgment must begin at the house of God: and if it first begin at us, what shall the end be of them that obey not the gospel of God? And if the righteous scarcely be saved, where shall the ungodly and the sinner appear?* 1 Peter 4:17-18

Dear friend, it is your responsibility today to choose Christ as your Savior and Lord. Make your calling and election sure, by knowing where you will go at the end of your short journey here on this planet earth.

Wendy Roberts chose Christ, and therefore when she breathed her last breath down here and opened her eyes, she was in the very presence of God. If you choose Him, you, too, will never be alone. *Never Alone!*   ✳

EPILOGUE

And he said unto me, My grace is sufficient for thee: for my strength is made perfect in weakness. Most gladly therefore will I rather glory in my infirmities, that the power of Christ may rest upon me.

2 Corinthians 12:9

It will be by God's grace that my life pleases Christ, for in the weakness of my spirit over the loss of Wendy it is only that grace that gives me the strength I need to carry on. I can't say that the pain of my loss has disappeared or that facing life without her has gotten somehow easy. What I can say is that God is faithful, and every day the burden gets lighter.

NEVER ALONE!

Wendy's life pleased Christ because of that same amazing grace. Grace will always overshadow the saint as a halo of love and peace to comfort and strengthen the soul. I know that one day all these wounds will be healed, and I will feel whole again. Until then, it is His grace that keeps me moving forward, and that same amazing grace can keep you.

It is God's grace that gives us spiritual energy through our prayer meetings and that give us the zeal we need for the mission to continue sending the needed food to those less fortunate. In our weakness, His grace and His presence will always be there, so we are not in this all by ourselves. No! We are *Never Alone!* ✳

A Son's Tribute

Dear Mom,

It's still so hard to believe that you're gone. It almost feels like yesterday when I saw you laughing, smiling and enjoying the blessed life that God had given you. I remember when I was small and you read me those classic books: *Around the World in 80 Days, The Three Musketeers, Oliver Twist* and *The Count of Monte Cristo*. I used to love hearing you narrate those stories in detail and with so much feeling.

Many people who knew you at your job saw you as a diligent, hard-working, persevering and motivated woman. There was another side to you though, and that was the loving, God-fearing, nurturing and compassionate woman. You taught me all about the Bible and about Jesus. You taught me all about that strong relationship with God that's so imperative to have, especially during the times we live in.

I remember those days when you used to dress me up in that nice white suit, as I was getting ready to go to church with you and Dad. You always used to say, "It's a very good thing to get dressed properly before you see God, because it represents the Spirit of God in you." I never forgot those words.

When it came to education, you always expected me to do my very best. I guess it's because you were an educator yourself. You always pushed me beyond my own limits. It's no wonder that in school I was always labeled as "white" or an "herb." When the rest of my peers were playing video games, staying up all night watching TV, or partying, I was at home studying for the next exam. When the other kids would make fun of me because I carried such a heavy book bag to school, you would dry my tears and encourage me, like the nurturing mother you were. You would always say to me, "Don't listen to them; they're ignorant and don't know any better."

You sometimes added, "Daniel, you will not be the next African-American male to 'bang out,' 'chill out' on the streets and not do anything with your life. We have too many Black males who are either in jail or dead because of the fact that they made very wrong choices." You toughened me up. You sharpened me for the next battle.

High school was a very difficult time for me because I had to deal with so much peer pressure. I remember the day I brought home my first bad grade on a report card. You said to me, "Daniel, what is this? Now I know for sure that you could've done much better." You were crushed when you saw that grade, but I promised to make it up to you. When I repeated that course during summer school, I received an A, and you were so proud. You said, "This is the kind of grade that I always want to see on your report card."

Still, there were to be more times when I would fail my courses as I went through a period of adolescent rebellion, but you were always so patient, so kind, and you kept paying for me to take courses in summer school. I thank you for that patience.

In 2002, during my senior year in high school, I heard through word of mouth that you had been diagnosed with breast cancer. You had done your best to hide that truth from me, but I still found out, and it broke me emotionally. Still, I refused to give in to my emotions. I promised myself that if the coming months were to be your last on earth, then I would excel in my studies during those months. And I passed my senior year with flying colors and graduated. Then how happy we all were when you received the doctor's report that you were miraculously healed!

During my year at Queensborough Community College, life couldn't have been better. I was majoring in the career of my choice, Principles of Accounting, and I joined my very first rock band and became its lead singer. Then two bad things happened: I received the report that your cancer had returned, and I was academically dismissed from QCC because my grades were down again. I thought my world had come to an end.

For the next two months, I did nothing but sulk and complain. Then you approached me about opportunities in the medical billing field. I said to you, "I'm not interested in medicine."

You answered, "Well you have two options: (1) Either go back or (2) Get a job. I'm not raising a young man who is in my house."

I decided to go back to school and, to my surprise, I excelled beyond my abilities again. I received the highest GPA in my classroom. I, then, did an internship at Mary Immaculate Hospital and received a job offer from them around the middle of August 2004. You congratulated me with hugs and kisses, making me feel as if I was the best son in the whole world. I was proud of myself, as well.

When I went back to college at Nassau Community College, it was a good time, although it was a difficult time because I knew that you were still going through chemotherapy, radiation and, finally, the removal of the cancerous breast. Even though I knew you were struggling physically, I still saw strength in you. I could see that this was one fight you were not planning to give in to any time soon. I admired that about you.

Life was starting to get better. I came out with my first music CD and said to you, "Mom, look at the talent that God has given me to write lyrics and record music. Isn't that great?"

You answered me, "Son, that's a very good talent to have, but always have a backup plan. You have to realize that you are one person going up against millions of other people. Jobs like these are not always guaranteed."

When I had my first girlfriend, I said to you, "Mom, she's such a jewel! I really care about her!"

You said to me, "Just make sure that if you're planning on marrying this woman, your finances are in order." I laughed at the time, yet I agreed.

On May 2007, you happily saw me graduate from NCC. I knew that God definitely had intervened for you to be alive to see both of these great achievements—my high school graduation and my college graduation. Then, as the months went by, I saw you battling a very different foe, as the cancer had metastasized into your lungs, causing you to have a hard time breathing. Doctors told you it was because you had smoked early in life, and you were so determined to warn all of your relatives who were still smoking.

As this drama gradually led to the end of your life, I sought to comfort you, speaking words that would calm you and make you think of the good and the positive. When you had heard those words, you were then at peace and you slept, calm and reassured that all would be all right.

When I saw you lying in that hospital bed, my father, I and a few good believers in Christ prayed for deliverance and healing. We thought that maybe some way, somehow you could be saved. It seemed that the Lord had a different plan in mind, and that was to give you the ultimate peace. I didn't understand this at first, and in my anger, I said, "Well if God is such a great God, why couldn't He heal my mother?" Then I remembered the scripture, *"For my thoughts are not your thoughts, neither are your ways my* *ways, saith the L*ORD*"* (Isaiah 55:8). Something good will come from this, Mother. I feel it in my spirit. Whatever God is doing in this situation will be great and marvelous in our eyes.

I want to tell you that I love you, I miss you and hope to see you again, either when I die or when the world ends— at God's own time. We know that to be absent from the body is to be present with the Lord (2 Corinthians 5:8). It makes me feel so good to know that your struggle is over and you're truly at peace.

Love you, Mother,
Daniel

MINISTRY PAGE

Readers may contact the author at the following addresses:

Daniel Roberts
Omega Outreach Ministries, Inc.
145–95 222nd Street
Springfield Gardens, NY 11413

email: danielrobers3@verizon.net
on the Internet: www.omegaoutreachministries.com

Printed in the United States
122141LV00003B/139-498/P